Copyright 2012 RETHINK (West) Inc.
Published by Lulu
ISBN# 978-1-300-23272-8

Photos from BizArt by Hemera
www.hemera.com

RETHINK (West) Inc.
5118 Brenton Page Road,
Ladysmith, BC V9G 1L6

www.rethink-group.com
250-245-8556

RETHINKING Governance

A Self-Assessment Tool and Action Planning
Handbook for the Non-Profit Board

Ken Balmer
Brenda Clarke

RETHINK (West) Inc.

Table of Contents

Acknowledgements 7

Preface 9

Section 1: Introducing the Framework 13

    Context 14
    Premises and Principles 16
    The RETHINKING Governance Framework 19

Section 2: The Assessment Tool 27

    How to Use the Tool 28
    Fiduciary Relationships 30
    Strategic Leadership 33
    Performance Assurance 36
    Stewardship and Sustainability 40
    Governance Policy and Process 42

Section 3: The Assessment Process 49

    Dimensions of Use 50
    Generalized Process Suggestions 52
    Graphic Summaries 54
    Action Plan 60

Section 4: Accountability and Role Clarity 61

    The Challenge 62
    The IRDEM Model 62
    The Board Calendar 69

Attachment 1: **References/Sources** 71

Acknowledgements

The authors share the learnings summarized in this book with our many clients who have risen to successfully address governance challenges. Over the past three decades, RETHINK has served over 200 board-directed organizations, each in its own way committed to leadership and adding value at the governance level. Our experience is theirs as well.

We are also indebted to the many authors and capacity building groups that have developed models, board evaluation tools, checklists and new governance theories. This audit handbook is founded on this extensive and growing body of work.

Finally, the authors acknowledge YOU the current reader. By simply picking up this handbook, you join the ever increasing numbers of volunteers and staff in the non-profit sector who are passionate about improving governance performance and outcomes.

> "There is no other way that as few people can raise the quality of the whole (American) Society as far and as fast as can trustees and directors of our voluntary organizations, using the strength they now have in the positions they now hold."
>
> Robert K. Greenleaf

Preface

What kind of board do you want to be?

Many Boards are content to meet a few times a year to review reports, plans and proposals brought forward by their CEO, CAO or Executive Director – clearly reactionary, often the 'rubber stamp' board.

Others combine this reactive, 'second view' role with a commitment to oversight. These boards establish mechanisms to check up on what is happening in the organization on a regular basis – often relying on personal judgement and undefined criteria in their assessment or critique.

Still others structure themselves to duplicate and monitor management functions. Member skill sets and committee structures read very much like the job description they have developed for their CEO/CAO/ED – finance, personnel, communications, and program.

> "Put together a group of strong-minded people, arrange for them to meet six times a year, have no performance targets for them, and recruit a number of outsiders with no knowledge of the industry or the company into the group. Would they function as a team? We doubt it. Yet this is how we organize (corporate) boards. They are thrown together half a dozen times a year, with vague -- sometimes nonexistent -- performance objectives and expected to provide decisive leadership and deliver corporate performance to exacting governance standards. Then we wonder why it sometimes goes wrong."
>
> Rob Goffee

All of these abovementioned boards are the ones that have led us to an ongoing governance crisis in the non-profit sector. These are the boards that their senior staffs view as 'necessary evils'. These boards have spawned both countless discussions about the value of a board and increasing interest in looking at alternatives, perhaps even doing away with these types of boards altogether. These boards are often seen as resource drains; the time spent servicing their questionable activities reduces the resources available for service impact – without adding value.

This handbook is not for those boards, unless they have decided to change. This book is for leadership boards that want to clearly add value to their organization, that want to define and deliver a unique contribution that can best be made at the governance level, and that want to do this work themselves – not simply adding more work to the responsibilities of their already beleaguered staff.

What is this handbook about?

The authors have crafted this handbook with three purposes in mind:
- To support constant improvement in non-profit board performance
- To identify and promote commitment to best practices, and
- To build stakeholder confidence in the work of non-profit boards and their organizations.

It focuses on board competencies, with practice guidelines and related quality indicators for each competency. The resulting list of practice guidelines goes far beyond the basics required by law and initial constitutions. This handbook focusses on governance roles and responsibilities. It only indirectly addresses the variety of board behaviours and interpersonal styles that ultimately determine function or dysfunction.

Essentially, you are holding a self-assessment tool and a guide to action planning to address competencies or related practices that require attention.

This handbook is prescriptive in the sense that it lists practice guidelines

Board Competencies and Related Practice Guidelines
- the 'value add' that creates a high performance board

Minimum Legal Obligations
- required by government legislation and common to all non-profit organizations
- some variation by jurisdiction

Board Behaviour
- Individual personalities and workstyles that nurture function or create dysfunction
- board culture

(or best practices) for each of five governance competency areas. Participating board members are asked to rate their performance against each of 30 practice guidelines. However, this evaluative work is customized to the unique character and needs of your organization, by encouraging you to reflect on the extent to which each practice guideline is really important or critical in your context.

Ultimately, the self-assessment tool facilitates identification of those practices where performance is rated low AND that participants believe are important. An action planning guide and role clarification model (IRDEM) is provided to help you improve board performance in these areas.

Who is the handbook written for?

This handbook targets those who want to optimize the time they spend with a board, either as trustee or staff.

The authors acknowledge the breadth and complexity of the board job description implied in this handbook. We don't expect immediate adoption of all of the practice guidelines recommended. We hope that concerned individuals and teams will use this resource to identify the critical few practices that need attention and strengthening at any given time in the development and evolution of your board.

You will find this handbook useful and instructive, as a guide to improvement, if you are:

> "What's fascinating about so many of the governance reformers is not that they are cynical about the role of boards, but that they are so idealistic. The notion that independent directors can, on a part-time basis, simultaneously and successfully formulate strategy, hire and fire senior executives, ensure rigid compliance with myriad global procedures, detect fraud, appropriately incentivize managerial performance, and oversee metrics for organizational performance, all without any actionable conflicts of interest, strikes me as exceedingly optimistic."
>
> Joel Kurtzman

- An individual board member who wants to more fully understand the challenge of governance and focus their own contribution

- A CEO, CAO or ED who is expected to help the board optimize time together and wants to facilitate a 'value add' approach that brings out the best possible contribution from his or her board

- A board that knows deep down that it is not performing to expectations – either the highest ambitions of board members themselves and/or those of key organizational stakeholders.

- A 'good to high' performance board that needs a self-assessment tool that goes well beyond the norm of evaluating board process and generalized roles/responsibilities.

In short, this resource is for those who believe in the potential and importance of governance and want to help deliver the promise of Board level leadership and accountability.

 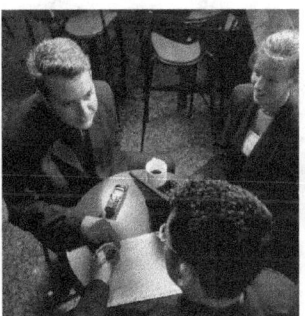 

Section 1:

Introducing the Framework

Context

Non-profit governance is a very large undertaking. In 2006, the National Study of Board Governance Practices in the Non-Profit and Voluntary Sector in Canada reported that the sector comprises 161,000 organizations, with some $112 billion in revenues annually, representing approximately 10% of Canada's gross domestic product.

Needless to say, all of this is governed by boards of directors who share a commitment to improving their own performance as well as the performance of their organizations. This commitment to enhanced governance plays out in a variety of ways:

- annual self-evaluation is now commonplace (for boards)
- individual board members are reading one or more of the books on governance that have emerged in the past couple of decades
- board development sessions are occurring more frequently, and
- capacity building organizations in almost every major urban area are supporting the efforts of individual non-profits to better understand and enhance governance theory and practice.

Despite all of this effort, the majority of these 161,000 boards still feel insecure, doubting that they are making the contribution or difference expected of strong leadership. Survey after survey of non-profit organizations repeatedly identifies governance as a critical issue.

> "The mandate of governance is to ensure that the organization delivers its promise of quality products and services; fulfills its mandate in a socially responsible manner; maintains financial viability and integrity; and has the requisite capacity to achieve a sustained level of high performance and ongoing responsiveness to its environment."
>
> Centre for Quality Governance, Toronto

Worse, many non-profit CEOs, CAOs and Executive Directors are even more concerned. The authors have heard many discussions framed by the realization that a board has become a drain on resources, not adding value in any significant way. These discussions search for alternative approaches that will make the governance effort worthwhile - for the board members themselves, senior staff that support them, and the organization's stakeholders. There is a fervent hope that boards will either reform and add value OR retreat to a marginalized, oversight role that allows the management team to focus on service and production.

And the job of governance is not getting any easier. The National Study of Board Governance Practices in the Non-Profit and Voluntary Sector in Canada (2006) identified a number of trends that are further challenging both our boards and the organizations they are responsible for (see table on next page).

Trends increasingly challenge our boards and organizations

Trends Challenging Boards	Trends Challenging Their Organizations
Increased focus on governance – increasing awareness of the importance of good governance and increasing sense of responsibility on the part of boards. **Increased demand for and reduced supply of qualified directors** - related to increasing litigiousness, demand for early retirees as board members, numbers of boards seeking directors, and emphasis on skills based boards.	**Changing demographics** – increase in required services, graying of the volunteer base, diversity of population **Shift in the funding environment** – greater demands for transparency and accountability from funders and donors, for information prior to funding – a shift from corporate philanthropy to sponsorship – a shift from operating support to project-based funding **More partnerships, networks and collaborations** **More charities and fewer people to lead** **Lack of resources** - directors, top talent, funds.

Source: Strategic Leverage Partners Inc. (see sources)

What have we learned?

As boards address these challenges, they are guided by a number of key lessons:

- boards now understand the need to shift from hands on interference or duplication of management functions to a focus on policy, strategy and performance assurance
- boards have learned to more clearly define when to pass the decision-making baton to the CEO, CAO or Executive Director
- John Carver taught boards the wisdom of focusing on definition of desired ends and then to free the staff racehorses to identify the best means to achieve these ends
- Corporate disasters in both the private and non-profit sectors have reminded boards of their fiduciary and financial responsibilities – of their ultimate responsibility as board members if the organizations they govern go off track
- Richard Chait taught us 'governance as leadership'.

Premises and Principles

'RETHINKING Governance' provides a framework for you and your organization to self-assess how your board is performing and to do something about any weak areas you discover during the process. The authors have not attempted to rethink governance itself; the rethinking happens at your end.

The governance model presented in this handbook is based on four key premises or principles:

- the desirability of shifting from 'hands on' governance (a duplication of management) to a 'value add' board role related to vision, policy, strategy and performance assurance
- the need for organizations to be more 'outcome driven' – focussed on the difference that the organization can make for the individuals and/or communities they serve
- a broader understanding of 'fiduciary responsibility' and stakeholder accountability
- Clear definition and separation of board and CEO/CAO/ED roles and responsibilities.

The Shift from 'Hands on' Governance

Very few contemporary boards are comfortable living in the left column of the table below. Only Boards that have few staff and must share the management load can justify this approach. Boards are doing their best to complete and/or maintain their shift to the right column behaviours.

Moving away from 'hands on' governance

From HANDS ON	Towards TRUE GOVERNANCE
Focus on DETAIL	Appreciation of BIG PICTURE
Focus on OPERATIONS/ACTIVITIES	Focus on OUTCOMES – results, difference made
Criticizing SMALL ISSUES	MONITORING PROGRESS toward desired outcomes
Obsessed with BUDGET LINES	FINANCIAL STEWARDSHIP and sustainability
ROWING – doing the work	STEERING or directing
Emphasis on CURRENT ISSUES	Focus on both current and EMERGING ISSUES
INTERNAL FOCUS on the organization	INTERNAL/EXTERNAL – owner and stakeholder liaison
REACTIVE decision-making	PROACTIVE/VISIONARY leadership
Committees DUPLICATE MANAGEMENT FUNCTIONS (finance, personnel, program)	Committees support BOARD WORK – policy, performance assurance, development, audit, etc.

Towards Outcome-Driven Organizations

Organizational planning systems have been evolving towards an emphasis on proven delivery of desired outcomes or results for over three decades:

- In the 1970's, MBR (Management by Results) replaced MBO (Management by Objectives)
- In the 1980's ZBB (Zero Based Budgeting) helped organizations question all assumptions about a program or service and required proof of value
- Late in the same decade, Business Re-Engineering challenged organizations to find new, modern ways to achieve desired results
- In the 1990's, logic models were adopted in virtually every context where a grant had to be applied for and accounted for, once spent – a new emphasis on outcomes
- In the same decade, John Carver's Policy Governance model promoted board focus on ends.

Boards everywhere have now accepted the challenge of defining the outcomes, ends or results desired. The most inspired Boards have worked with their CEO/CAO/ED to build an outcome culture in their organizations.

The Outcome-Driven Organization

From SERVICE-DRIVEN	Towards OUTCOME-DRIVEN
Goals and objectives for each program	Ends/outcomes for organization - programs deliver
CEO/CAO/ED evaluated on efficiency	CEO/CAO/ED evaluated primarily on outcome delivery
Plans respond to wants	Plans find best ways to deliver outcomes
Modify existing services to increase efficiency & customer satisfaction	Modify services to more effectively address desired outcomes and customer benefits
Market research to determine wants	Market research to identify priority outcomes/benefits
Expand services that sell well	Expand services that have proven outcome delivery
Commitment to programs/services	Willing to change a 'sacred cow' if a better way of achieving desired outcomes can be found
Staff hired for program skills	Staff hired for commitment to desired outcomes
Evaluation on outputs/efficiency/satisfaction	Evaluation also measures outcome achievement
Bottom line and efficiency focus	Willing to spend a little more to get outcome desired
Somewhat isolationist and competitive	Willing to partner with others to better deliver outcomes
Annual reporting based on activities	Annual reporting of results, outcomes, difference made

Fiduciary Responsibility in the 21st Century

For over a century, non-profit boards have been required by law to owe an obligation of trust to the organization's stakeholders. Boards perform on behalf of a moral ownership, members (often also service recipients), and investors/funders. This requirement has been reinforced in modern governance literature:

- John Carver, in his book 'Boards That Make a Difference', summarized three job products of the board. The first was: "linkage to the ownership – the board acts in trusteeship for ownership and services as the legitimizing connection between this base and the organization."

- The first guideline for high performance boards proposed by the Canadian Coalition for Good Governance is "to facilitate shareholder democracy" – admittedly a corporate model where individual shareholders have the right to vote their shares, but easily transferable as a principle to the non-profit world
- Chait, Ryan and Taylor in their remarkable book, 'Governance as Leadership', speak of Type 1 governance focused on fiduciary work, the foundation upon which strategic and generative work is added.

However, over the years the word 'fiduciary' has been somewhat narrowly defined through the eyes of accountants and lawyers. Boards have begun to see this task as managing the financial and asset resources of the organization, much the way a fiduciary trustee of a fund would be expected to perform. Chait, Ryan and Taylor have broadened the concept in their model to include virtually all of the standard board functions excepting those related to strategy, planning and foresight. When those authors speak of the shift from fiduciary oversight to fiduciary enquiry, they challenge boards to broaden their view of fiduciary responsibility – embracing financial, strategic, resource allocation and development domains.

The broader view taken in this handbook is that modern fiduciary responsibility encompasses all that a board undertakes to develop, ensure and protect value to its owners and stakeholders. Those that place board members in a position of trust to act on their behalf are not only thinking of the finances and assets; they also expect the board to create and enforce a high performance culture that delivers against organizational promise, potential and priorities.

Clear Definition of Board and CEO/CAO/ED Responsibilities

While there are many variables to consider in defining the relative roles of the board and its staff leadership team, the table below summarizes the assumptions that the RETHINKING Governance Framework has been built around.

Board/CEO Roles and Responsibilities

Key Roles of the BOARD	Key Roles of the CEO/ED
Understand and represent stakeholder priorities Define Outcomes or Results expected Define business parameters (focus and values)	Conduct stakeholder research, surveys, needs assessments Develop and manage strategies and tactics to deliver outcomes Allocate and manage resources within defined parameters
Long Range strategic and financial planning	Support long range planning Short/medium term business and operational planning
Board to Board relations (gov., funders, partners)	Develop and support operational strategic alliances
Audit and monitor progress toward outcomes, financial goals and strategic priorities	Manage monitoring system and report on progress – ensure that management team acts on performance management info
Create and adhere to governance model	Support and build mechanisms to nurture trust and confidence in the governance model
Hire, support and evaluate the CEO/ED	Attract and nurture a high performance team (both staff and volunteer)

The Framework

The 'RETHINKING Governance' Framework is based on five critical questions:

- Has the board developed relationships with the organization's owners and stakeholders that allow it to credibly act on their behalf?
- Does the board add strategic leadership value to direct and position the organization in an increasingly demanding and competitive operating environment?
- Has the board developed the capacity to effectively monitor and enhance delivery of the organization's value and promise to stakeholders?
- Does the board understand and act on its ultimate responsibility for the organization's long term health, wellbeing and sustainability?
- Has the board developed policies, processes and the discipline to focus its own efforts on key governance roles and responsibilities?

Each of the above questions identifies one of five core governance competencies – summarized in the graphic below.

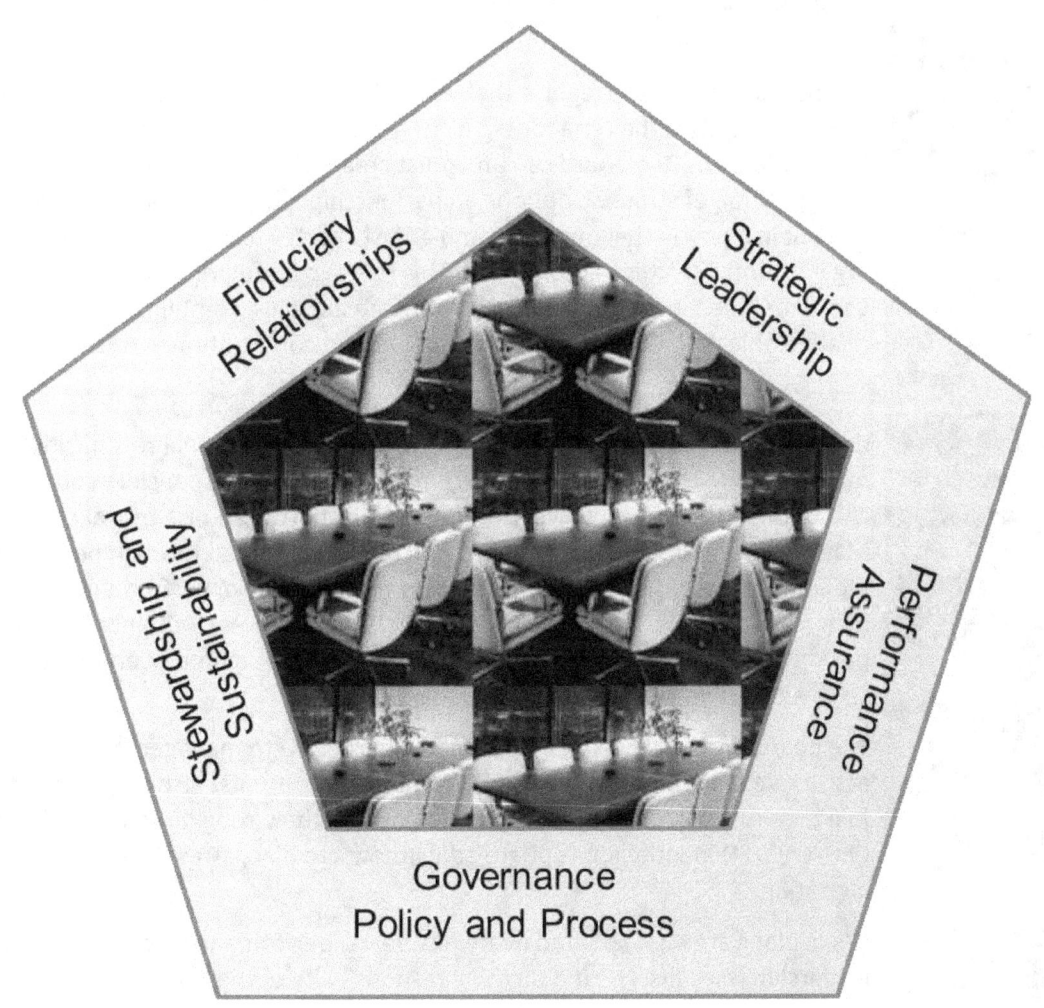

Competency Domain Overview

Fiduciary Relationships	This domain is not about responsibilities (they cover the gamut), only about relationships. The board is required by law to act on behalf of its owners, represent stakeholders and carry the public trust. Often the ownership is a moral ownership – a target population whose special needs are to be served by the organization. How can this obligation be truly respected without board insight and knowledge about its key constituents? Given current emphasis on recruiting members with appropriate skill sets, boards must learn about and ensure engagement with those who truly understand the needs and interests of the owners. More effort is required to establish ongoing and meaningful interaction with key stakeholders. The arrogant board assumes it knows; the responsible board finds out.
Strategic Leadership	The board holds ultimate responsibility for determining the purpose, perimeter or scope of concern, visionary outcomes, operating philosophy, overall direction and strategic priorities of the organization. These responsibilities can be shared with the CEO/CAO/ED, but never fully delegated. The board must ensure that organizational purpose, vision, mandate, culture and positioning is responsive to changes in the operating environment. The board must also recognize that its staff is often mired in administration and challenged to find the time for big picture thinking and management, let alone true leadership. The board can and must create the space for reflection and consideration of strategic options, in partnership with its management team. It must help develop the long view, and adjust shorter term priorities and organizational strategy accordingly. This role is particularly important when board members have the visionary and strategic skills, combined with their relative objectivity, to make a unique value-add contribution.
Performance Assurance	Contemporary boards delegate the majority of organizational responsibilities to management. However, the board remains ultimately responsible and accountable for overall delivery of the organization's promise to stakeholders. Many of the board's fiduciary responsibilities are handled through performance monitoring related to meeting legal obligations, financial performance, key HR factors, and reputation. The board must also monitor performance to plan, performance to strategy, progress towards desired outcomes, service quality and service effectiveness/efficiency. The board must provide an accountability structure to management and take an active role in monitoring macro or key indicators. It must also be prepared to join the discussion when indicators are going in the wrong direction, helping the CEO/CAO/ED identify appropriate adjustments to plan, strategy and resource allocation. While plans are best updated every few years; performance monitoring and leadership is a constant and ongoing responsibility of the Board.

Stewardship and Sustainability	While day-to-day management responsibilities are generally delegated to the management team, the board retains ultimate responsibility for the organization's long term health and well-being – for stewardship of the organization and its assets. This stewardship role extends far beyond finances to include protection of human resource, physical and reputational assets. Clearly this key role also obliges the board to take an active, high level role (along with the CEO) in the identification, evaluation and management of business risk. The stewardship and sustainability lens must be applied to every board decision making process.
Governance Policy and Process	The board must also govern itself. It is obliged to develop, maintain and respect both policy and processes that ensure meaningful and substantive action: • in each of the above governance competency domains • to meet obligations defined in the organization's charter and constitution • to constantly improve its own governance performance.

"If management is about running the business, governance is about seeing that it is run properly."

R. Tricker

"An attempt must be made to define where the institution wants to go, how and when it will arrive there, with whom it will travel, and what the cost of the trip will be."

Rhoda M. Dorsey

"A good board member must be able to face budgets with courage, endowments with doubt, deficits with dismay, and to recover quickly from a surplus."

Michael Davis

"A good board member should be part of a tradition but eager to improve it."

Michael Davis

Fleshing out the Model

Although the framework is structured around five Governance Competency Domains, they are not specific enough to support a valid self-assessment process. Five Practice Guidelines have been developed for the first four domains; ten additional Practice Guidelines support the Governance Policy/Process domain. Your self-assessment therefore considers a total of 30 Practice Guidelines.

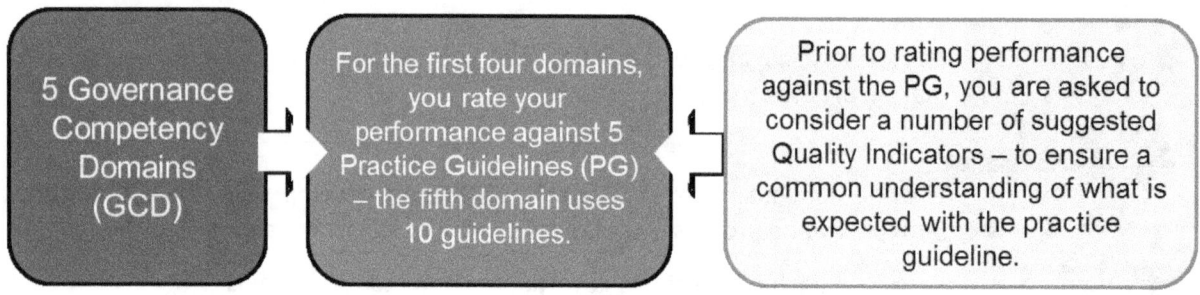

The following five diagrams summarize the 30 Practice Guidelines that comprise the self-assessment tool.

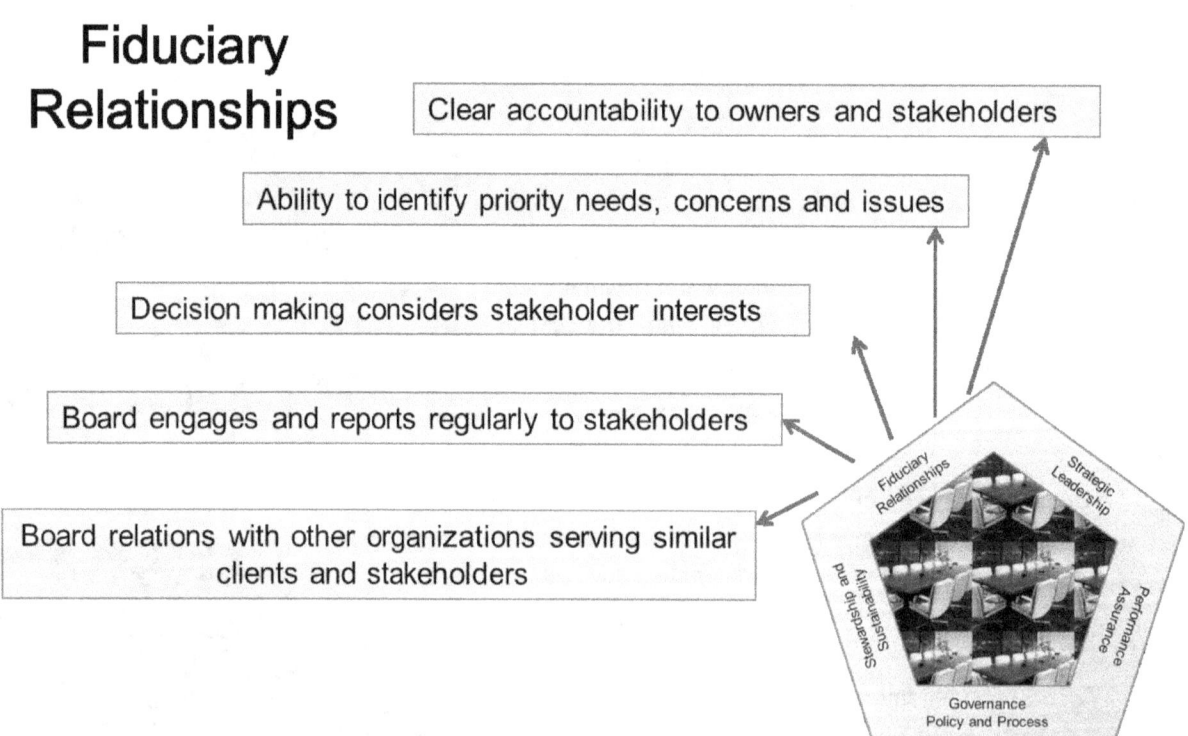

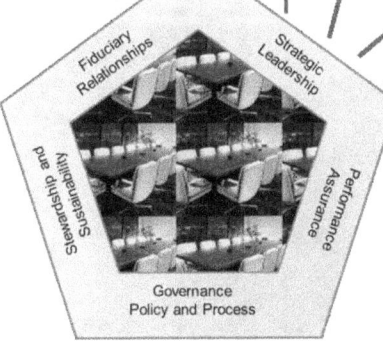

- Clear purpose, vision, focus and perimeter of concern
- Well defined priorities and strategic direction
- Support for constant improvement and innovation
- Champion of the organization's brand and reputation
- Development/refinement of organizational strategy

Strategic Leadership

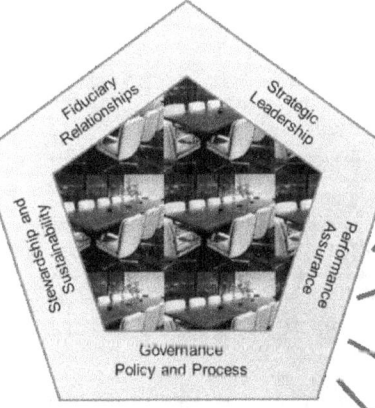

- Building an outcome-driven culture
- Monitoring/evaluating delivery of outcomes
- Regular reports on performance to budget, productivity/efficiency and service quality
- CEO/CAO/ED performance management
- Annual financial audit of organizational performance

Performance Assurance

Stewardship and Sustainability

- Long range financial plans and strategies
- Board leadership in fund development program
- Protection of human resource assets
- Comprehensive asset management program
- Policies and processes to manage business risk

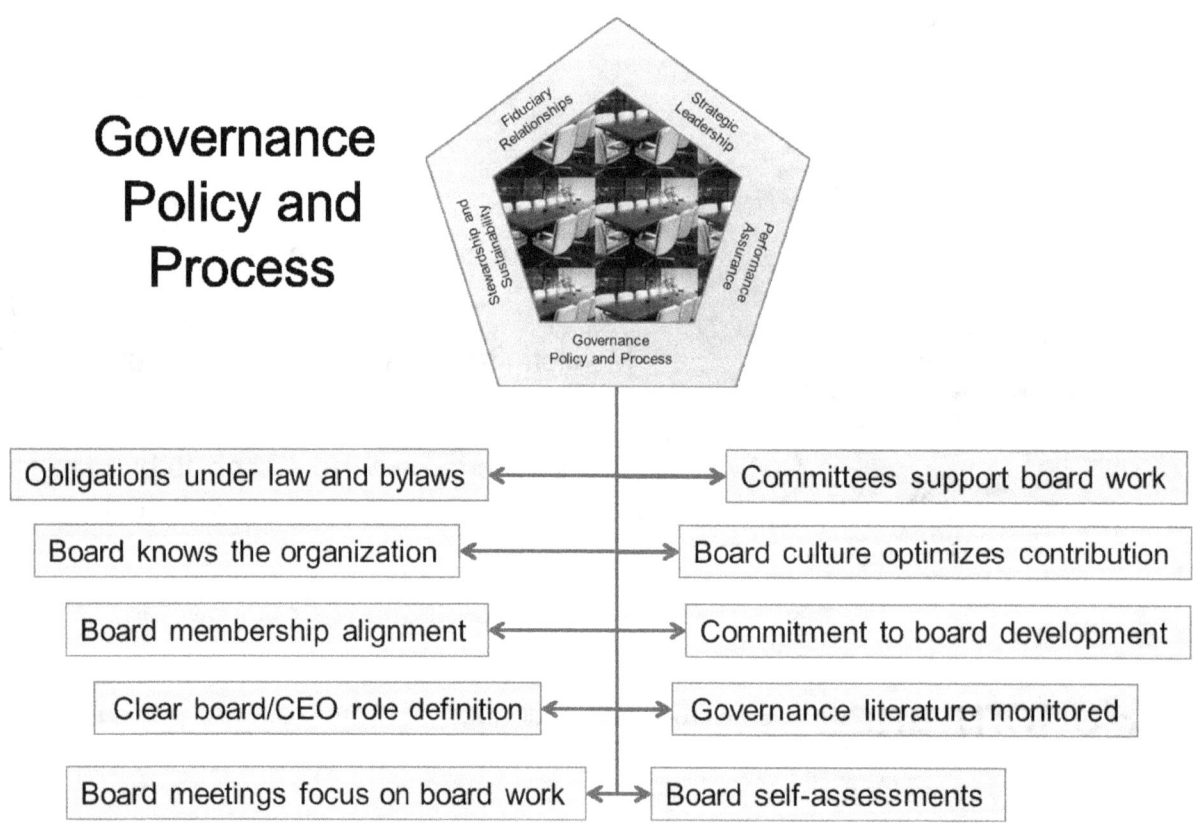

Governance Policy and Process

- Obligations under law and bylaws
- Board knows the organization
- Board membership alignment
- Clear board/CEO role definition
- Board meetings focus on board work
- Committees support board work
- Board culture optimizes contribution
- Commitment to board development
- Governance literature monitored
- Board self-assessments

Section 2 contains the self-assessment tool that provides Quality Indicators for each of the 30 practice statements shown in the graphics above.

Self-Assessment or Audit

As both consultants and authors, we are well aware of the trepidation that many organizations, or individual leaders, experience when faced with an assessment or audit. While we are sympathetic, we also believe there is no way to avoid the uncomfortable feelings that accompany the scrutiny that always precedes improvement. The trick is to simply make the process as non-threatening as possible.

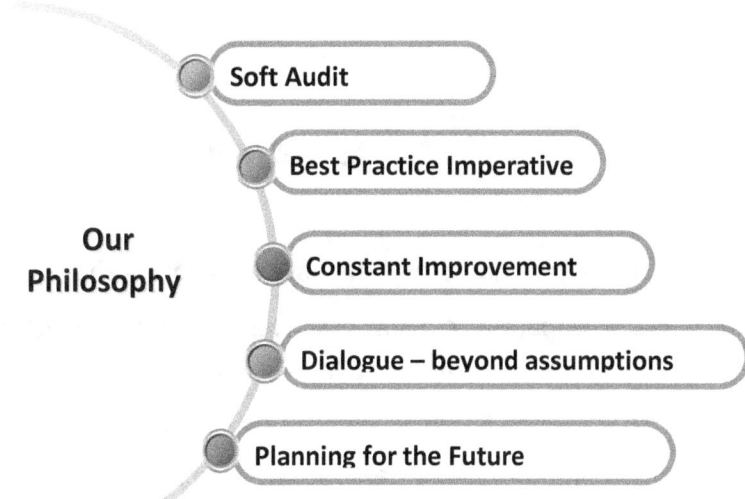

Soft Audit	Ideally, you and your colleagues will view this tool and process as a 'soft' audit. It will not follow the traditional financial audit purpose of examining carefully with the intent of verification, by an external examiner. It will be a self-assessment; you will have full control over the process and how results are utilized or shared. It will be exploratory rather than judgmental. But it will remain a methodological examination of the condition or standard of your governance enterprise.
Best Practice Imperative	The authors believe that the individual member or Board is foolish to ignore established understandings of the best way to go about handling the leadership role you have accepted. While all might entertain some ambition to innovate and lead, the harsh reality is that few will ever rise to that plateau of excellence. We hold the belief that there is always a preferred method of achieving a desired result. We respect well-defined procedures that are known to produce near-optimum outcomes. And we believe that in most cases, these operational procedures have already been discovered and tested, though still evolving.
Constant Improvement	If your governance policies and processes are relatively immature, going through an assessment or soft audit process may be more than daunting, perhaps even overwhelming. In this situation, believe in the Japanese concept of Kaizen: a philosophy that embraces constant, incremental improvement towards ever higher quality standards. Start from where you find yourself and maintain a commitment to continuous enhancement. Commit to the first step; then keep moving forward!
Dialogue – beyond assumptions	Perhaps the most significant value of a soft audit process is the fact that it will be a conversation starter. You will find differences in perceptions, level of knowledge, views of the evaluative criteria themselves. The understanding and potential for new consensus that will come from simply engaging in the dialogue required to get Board members on the same page will justify your investment in the process.
Planning for the Future	We also endorse the wisdom of the ancient Chinese proverb: "If you are planning for a year, sow rice; if you are planning for a decade, plant trees; but if you are planning for the future, educate your children." We know that this assessment or soft audit tool will help you find priorities as you plan for short, medium and long term improvement to your governance practices and performance.

SELF-ASSESSMENT will help your Board:

- ❏ better understand the nature of comprehensive, governance leadership
- ❏ compare its current practices with accepted governance theory and best practice literature– gap analysis
- ❏ establish a benchmark for future tracking
- ❏ compare/clarify perspectives and assumptions about what is happening in your organization
- ❏ identify gaps, issues or challenges that should be addressed
- ❏ establish a framework for future governance efforts and ventures – positioning for a higher level of governance performance
- ❏ establish priorities, and
- ❏ ultimately, develop a customized governance approach and set of practices appropriate to your organization's context, capacity and challenges.

Section 2:

The Assessment Tool

Go ahead and use the self-assessment tool right now – there is no better way to understand it, than to actually experience it!

How to use the assessment tool

You will be working with the 5 Governance Competency Domains captured in the framework. Each domain is further explained through 5 Practice Guidelines, each gleaned from the rather extensive board self-evaluation literature. Prior to rating each of the Practice Guidelines, you are asked to review a number of Quality Indicators to provide a better feel for what the guidelines implies.

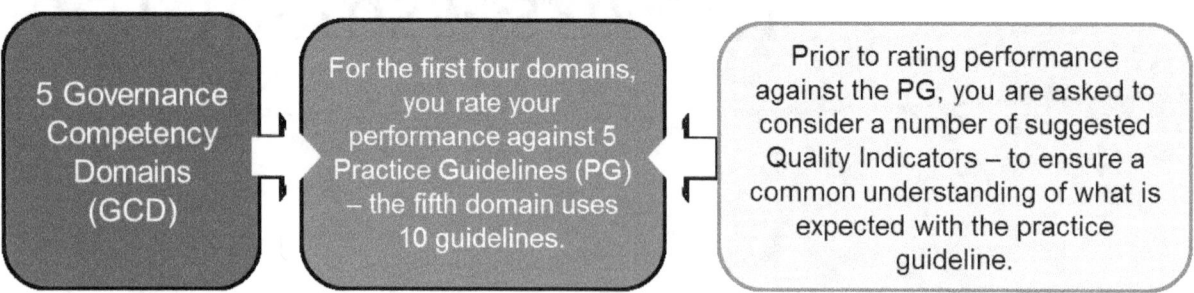

Work your way through the assessment tool one practice guideline at a time. In each case:

- review the set of Quality Indicators for the guidelines, thinking about actual activities of your board over the past 2 to 3 years
- place a tick mark in the box beside any Quality Indicator that sounds like you Board or reflects your organization's operations – use an 'X' to indicate any that are not followed by your Board or in your organization – use a '?' beside any Quality Indicators that you want to explore further before finalizing your rating
- then return to the Practice Guideline and circle your rating on the 7-point scale outlined below.

Rating Overall Success and Performance: The following rating scale definitions can be used to assess your overall success and performance with each practice guideline:

7 –	**Excellent**	The Board consistently addresses all the Quality Indicators, and even more
6 -	**Very Good**	For the most part, the Board addresses all the Quality Indicators
5 -	**Good**	Most of the Quality Indicators are addressed, but with some inconsistency
4 –	**OK/Average**	The Board only consistently addresses about 50% of the Quality Indicators
3 –	**Weak**	The Board addresses a few of the Quality Indicators, with inconsistency
2 –	**Poor**	The Board intends to address the Quality Indicators but has trouble finding time/resources
1 -	**Unacceptable**	The Board does not get around to it; failure to deliver the service.

If you don't know enough to rate the practice guideline, circle DK (don't know) at the bottom of the box.

Generally, if most of the Quality Indicators for the Practice Guideline have a tick mark, you would give your organization a high rating (e.g. 5-7). If there are not many tick marks, you would normally give your organization a lower rating. The rating will be a judgement: you may have tick marks but not really be satisfied with performance in each of those areas; alternatively, you may have a number of 'works in progress' that do not justify a tick mark at this time, but suggest a strong commitment to the Practice Guideline. Each individual will provide a rating based on his or her assumptions; assumptions that will be clarified during the very valuable discussions that follow a low average rating by the governance team.

Space is provided to make a comment that either explains your rating or provides a suggestion for improving the situation.

Rating Level of Importance: Before you move on to the next Practice Guideline, please consider the importance of the Practice Guideline in the context of your organization. The authors anticipate that you will want to see the majority of the Practice Guidelines in operation for your board and organization – therefore indicating 'high importance'. However, some may not be important to you for a variety of reasons and therefore be designated as 'low importance'. Possible reasons for a 'low importance' rating include:

- this practice has been fully and formally delegated to our CEO/CAOED – the board's only role is to monitor as part of their performance assurance work
- this practice conflicts with the governance approach and philosophy of the organization
- in the Board's view, this is simply not a critical function and is not worth the effort.

Please use the following Likert Scale to rate the importance of the PG in your organizational context:

Not at all important   1 2 3 4 5 6 7   **Very Important**
(no need to worry about it)   (we must perform well in this area)

Space is again provided for your comment or explanation. Please be sure to provide a rationale for any Practice Guidelines that you rated as 1, 2 or 3.

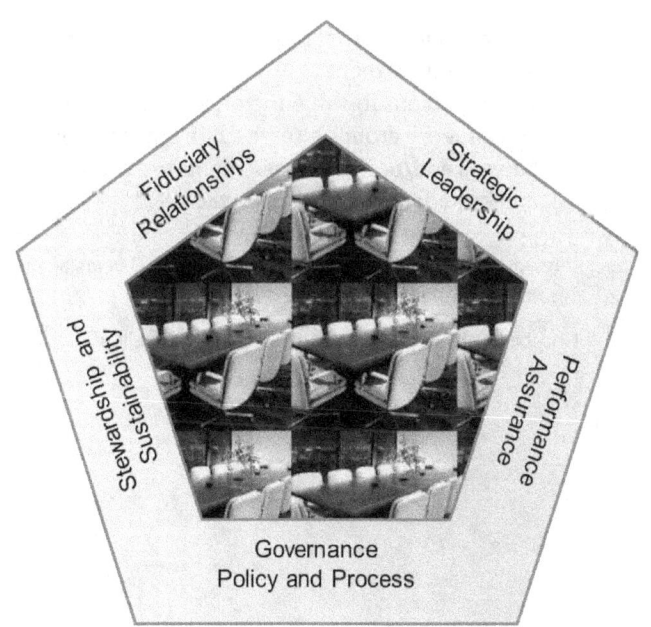

1 – Fiduciary Relationships

Practice Guideline 1.1:
The Board understands and acts on its accountability to its owners and stakeholders.

Quality Indicators to consider prior to rating this Practice Guideline:

- ☐ The Board has identified to whom it is ultimately accountable (the owners, members, moral ownership)
- ☐ Board policies clearly identify the organization's priority constituency groups and clarify who is responsible for understanding and building relationships with each group.
- ☐ The Board reports at least annually to these stakeholders
- ☐ The Annual Meeting provides for and facilitates effective stakeholder understanding and critique of the organization's policies, plans and services.
- ☐ Stakeholders have the ability and opportunity to influence Board member elections or appointments.

Rate your **overall performance** over the past 2-3 years against this Practice Guideline: Unacceptable 1 2 3 4 5 6 7 Excellent Comments: DK	Rate the **importance** of practicing this Guideline in your organizational context: Not at all 1 2 3 4 5 6 7 Very Comments:

Practice Guideline 1.2:
The Board has developed mechanisms and strategies for regularly identifying the priority needs, concerns and issues of the organization's key stakeholders.

Quality Indicators to consider prior to rating this Practice Guideline:

- ☐ Board planning processes include input and involvement by those to whom the Board is accountable, as well as relevant partners.
- ☐ The Board ensures that the organization maintains profiles, inventories and assessments on the constituency groups it serves with emphasis on monitoring changes and identifying service gaps
- ☐ Surveys and/or needs assessments are conducted from time to time to identify stakeholder, customer and/or service recipient priorities.

Rate your **overall performance** over the past 2-3 years against this Practice Guideline: Unacceptable 1 2 3 4 5 6 7 Excellent Comments: DK	Rate the **importance** of practicing this Guideline in your organizational context: Not at all 1 2 3 4 5 6 7 Very Comments:

Practice Guideline 1.3:
Board decision making processes are designed to practice inclusion of stakeholder interests and ensure delivery of the organization's unique value proposition to each target audience.

Quality Indicators to consider prior to rating this Practice Guideline:

- ☐ The Board consistently steps back prior to taking significant decisions to ask how key constituency groups would view the issue and options available.
- ☐ The Board has clearly defined the value proposition that the organization delivers to each target audience or constituency group and checks to ensure that each major policy decision supports the delivery process.
- ☐ Prior to major decisions, opportunities are provided for input from those most affected.

Rate your **overall performance** over the past 2-3 years against this Practice Guideline:	Rate the **importance** of practicing this Guideline in your organizational context:
Unacceptable 1 2 3 4 5 6 7 Excellent	Not at all 1 2 3 4 5 6 7 Very
Comments:	Comments:
DK	

Practice Guideline 1.4:
The Board engages and reports regularly to its stakeholders.

Quality Indicators to consider prior to rating this Practice Guideline:

- ☐ Board processes are open and transparent; encouraging and facilitating stakeholder input.
- ☐ The Board utilizes multiple channels to communicate with key stakeholders (print, web site, surveys prior to key decisions, circulation of draft plans/policies, etc.)
- ☐ Interactive channels are preferred – two way communication
- ☐ A 'plain language' Annual Report reports on progress, shows clearly how the organization has used its resources, summarizes the challenges facing the organization, identifies priorities for the coming year, and invites input/feedback.

Rate your **overall performance** over the past 2-3 years against this Practice Guideline:	Rate the **importance** of practicing this Guideline in your organizational context:
Unacceptable 1 2 3 4 5 6 7 Excellent	Not at all 1 2 3 4 5 6 7 Very
Comments:	Comments:
DK	

Practice Guideline 1.5:
The Board has developed relationships with other organizations that serve similar clients/stakeholders, driven by similar outcomes – towards networked, collaborative effectiveness.

Quality Indicators to consider prior to rating this Practice Guideline:

☐ The Board has identified related organizations that have a mandate to serve the same constituency groups or target groups.
☐ These groups are consulted during major planning initiatives or processes.
☐ Board to Board discussions are held from time to time to share experience and explore collaborative options that would better serve shared clients.
☐ The Board looks for opportunities to work with these organizations in areas of common interest, such as needs assessments, public policy development, and advocacy.

Rate your **overall performance** over the past 2-3 years against this Practice Guideline: Unacceptable 1 2 3 4 5 6 7 Excellent Comments: DK	Rate the **importance** of practicing this Guideline in your organizational context: Not at all 1 2 3 4 5 6 7 Very Comments:

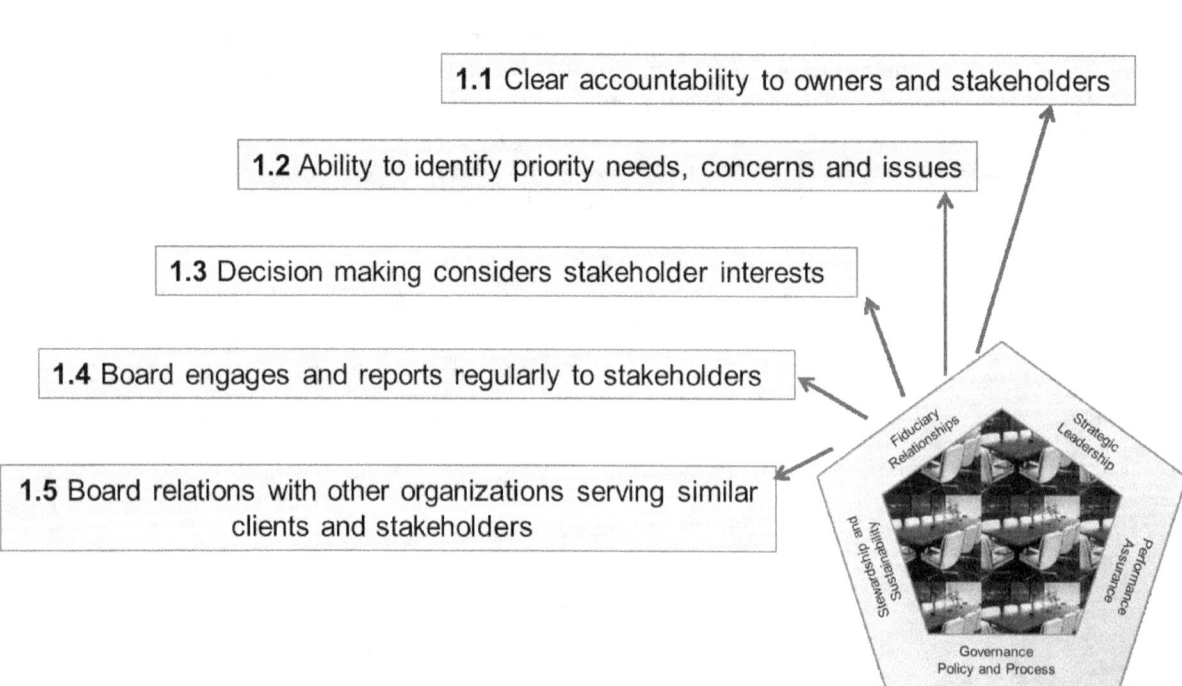

2 – Strategic Leadership

Practice Guideline 2.1:
The Board has clearly defined the purpose of the organization, its focus and perimeter of concern.

Quality Indicators to consider prior to rating this Practice Guideline:

- ☐ The Board has approved high level policies that define organizational purpose (mission, vision, desired outcomes).
- ☐ The Board has approved high level policies that define operational focus and perimeter of concern (priority clients/customers, geographic area of influence, core services/businesses).
- ☐ The Board has disciplined itself to align all of its policies, plans and decisions with these purpose, focus and perimeter of concern statements.

Rate your **overall performance** over the past 2-3 years against this Practice Guideline:	Rate the **importance** of practicing this Guideline in your organizational context:
Unacceptable 1 2 3 4 5 6 7 Excellent	Not at all 1 2 3 4 5 6 7 Very
Comments:	Comments:
DK	

Practice Guideline 2.2:
The Board is actively engaged in defining the organization's priorities and strategic direction.

Quality Indicators to consider prior to rating this Practice Guideline:

- ☐ The Board understands that it is responsible for identifying the long term vision and strategic direction of the organization.
- ☐ The board has worked with the CEO/ED to develop a strategic and/or business plan that defines direction and general organizational strategy for three to five years.
- ☐ Within this planning framework, the Board annually identifies priorities for the year or two ahead.
- ☐ The Board requires the CEO/ED to develop success Indicators and action plans for each priority and to report regularly on related progress (e.g. every quarter).

Rate your **overall performance** over the past 2-3 years against this Practice Guideline:	Rate the **importance** of practicing this Guideline in your organizational context:
Unacceptable 1 2 3 4 5 6 7 Excellent	Not at all 1 2 3 4 5 6 7 Very
Comments:	Comments:
DK	

Practice Guideline 2.3:
The Board understands the change imperative and supports organizational reflection, evaluation, constant improvement, and innovation.

Quality Indicators to consider prior to rating this Practice Guideline:

- ☐ The Board operates with foresight and has established processes to monitor trends and shifts in the organization's operating environment – and to think strategically about their implications and how best to respond.
- ☐ The Board protects the time to engage in exploratory and generative discussion.
- ☐ The Board encourages organizational exploration of options, alternatives and innovation to improve performance to mission and vision, and find better ways to achieve desired results or outcomes.
- ☐ The Board takes time to reflect on the fundamental paradigm shifts that are affecting virtually every aspect of society – to anticipate long term implications of these changes or shifts for the organization.

Rate your **overall performance** over the past 2-3 years against this Practice Guideline:	Rate the **importance** of practicing this Guideline in your organizational context:
Unacceptable 1 2 3 4 5 6 7 Excellent	Not at all 1 2 3 4 5 6 7 Very
Comments:	Comments:
DK	

Practice Guideline 2.4:
The Board is actively involved in defining, shaping, reinforcing and promoting the organization's brand and reputation.

Quality Indicators to consider prior to rating this Practice Guideline:

- ☐ The Board provides leadership in developing and establishing a clear positioning statement and brand for the organization.
- ☐ The Board consciously and deliberately behaves in a manner that demonstrates and exemplifies brand.
- ☐ The Board considers reputational risks each time a major decision is taken.
- ☐ Board members are aware of key messages and take advantage of every opportunity to use these in promoting the organization.
- ☐ Board members monitor organizational behaviours and question any that seem inconsistent with brand and desired positioning.
- ☐ The Board requires that the organization review the views of stakeholders about brand attributes every few years.

Rate your **overall performance** over the past 2-3 years against this Practice Guideline:	Rate the **importance** of practicing this Guideline in your organizational context:
Unacceptable 1 2 3 4 5 6 7 Excellent	Not at all 1 2 3 4 5 6 7 Very
Comments:	Comments:
DK	

Practice Guideline 2.5:
The Board reviews, discusses and debates organizational strategy designed to optimize all of the above commitments and practices.

Quality Indicators to consider prior to rating this Practice Guideline:

- ☐ The Board and CEO/CAO/ED agree on the organization's business model and regularly checks to ensure that all activities (both programmatic and support) advance delivery of value propositions to priority target markets and customers.
- ☐ Core organizational competencies are understood, protected, supported and enhanced to ensure competitive advantage
- ☐ The organization's unique value proposition for each constituency group is understood, protected, supported and enhanced to ensure customer satisfaction
- ☐ Traditional ways of doing business are reviewed, even challenged periodically to avoid counterproductive ruts.
- ☐ Systemic and cultural barriers to effective delivery of the organization's promise are identified and addressed.
- ☐ Discussion of alternative approaches and scenarios is encouraged.
- ☐ The Board is constantly searching for ideas that will improve performance to mission and vision.

Rate your **overall performance** over the past 2-3 years against this Practice Guideline:	Rate the **importance** of practicing this Guideline in your organizational context:
Unacceptable 1 2 3 4 5 6 7 Excellent	Not at all 1 2 3 4 5 6 7 Very
Comments:	Comments:
DK	

2.1 Clear purpose, vision, focus and perimeter of concern

2.2 Well defined priorities and strategic direction

2.3 Support for constant improvement and innovation

2.4 Champion of the organization's brand and reputation

2.5 Development/refinement of organizational strategy

3 – Performance Assurance

Practice Guideline 3.1:
The Board is actively engaged in the collaborative effort required to build an outcome-driven organization.

Quality Indicators to consider prior to rating this Practice Guideline:
- ☐ The strategic vision for the organization has been translated into visionary outcomes, intermediate outcomes and related indicators for the Board to monitor.
- ☐ The Board requires that all plans, budgets and monitoring systems focus in part on the delivery of these outcomes to the stakeholders and communities served by the organization.
- ☐ The Board encourages service modification and innovation to find ways to more effectively deliver the outcomes or results desired – flexible on the means but not the ends.
- ☐ The Board requires the organization to work with stakeholder and constituency groups to identify the priority outcomes desired by each.
- ☐ The CEO/ED is hired in large part based on his or her understanding of and commitment to the outcomes desired by the Board.
- ☐ The Board has made it clear that it is willing to partner with or devolve service to another organization if client based outcomes can be better delivered together or elsewhere.

Rate your **overall performance** over the past 2-3 years against this Practice Guideline:

Unacceptable 1 2 3 4 5 6 7 Excellent

Comments:

DK

Rate the **importance** of practicing this Guideline in your organizational context:

Not at all 1 2 3 4 5 6 7 Very

Comments:

Practice Guideline 3.2:
Processes are in place to monitor and evaluate the organization's ability to deliver promised outcomes and results – and to take appropriate governance action if progress is deemed insufficient.

Quality Indicators to consider prior to rating this Practice Guideline:
- ☐ The Board requires that high level or visionary outcomes (approved at the Board level) be translated into more specific and measurable outcomes to each program or service.
- ☐ A layered performance reporting system is in place delivering high level outcome measures to the Board (related to mission, visionary outcome, strategic priorities), measures of overall organizational performance to the CEO and management team, and more specific operational measures to each member of that team.
- ☐ Each time a measure or indicator is headed in the wrong direction, a brief report is provided outlining corrective action taken to date and suggesting longer term corrective strategy.
- ☐ The Board, from time to time, makes suggestions designed to better align organizational resources with priority outcomes.

Rate your **overall performance** over the past 2-3 years against this Practice Guideline:

Unacceptable 1 2 3 4 5 6 7 Excellent

Comments:

DK

Rate the **importance** of practicing this Guideline in your organizational context:

Not at all 1 2 3 4 5 6 7 Very

Comments:

Practice Guideline 3.3:

The Board receives reports (at least annually) on performance to budget, productivity/efficiency, and service quality – and intervenes appropriately when issues are identified.

Quality Indicators to consider prior to rating this Practice Guideline:

- ☐ The Board receives the information it needs to monitor the organization's financial health/stability, progress towards financial goals and targets.
- ☐ The Board receives the information it needs to ensure that financial and human resources are aligned with the organization's mission, desired outcomes and strategic priorities.
- ☐ Board members are financially literate, capable of understanding budget and audit reports.
- ☐ The Board ensures that the organization has the required financial management expertise and experience.
- ☐ When financial issues are identified the Board finds ways to provide input and advice to the CEO/ED without taking over related management roles and responsibilities.

Rate your **overall performance** over the past 2-3 years against this Practice Guideline:	Rate the **importance** of practicing this Guideline in your organizational context:
Unacceptable 1 2 3 4 5 6 7 Excellent	Not at all 1 2 3 4 5 6 7 Very
Comments:	Comments:
DK	

Practice Guideline 3.4:

The Board has defined and follows formal processes for managing CEO/CAO/ED performance.

Quality Indicators to consider prior to rating this Practice Guideline:

- ☐ The Board has developed CEO/CAO/ED supervision processes that include goal setting, coaching, monitoring/evaluating, and recognition/correction.
- ☐ The Board has developed a position description for the CEO/CAO/ED that includes both short and long term performance expectations or targets, and related indicators.
- ☐ The Board has developed formal criteria and a process for evaluating the CEO/CAO/ED.
- ☐ The Board evaluates the CEO/ED primarily on the accomplishment of the outcomes, goals and targets identified in Board policy and plans.
- ☐ An annual CEO/CAO/ED performance evaluation is conducted that seeks input from Board members, senior staff, partners and funders. The evaluation reviews outcome achievement, performance to board approved strategy and priorities, supervision of critical management functions, and contribution to organizational reputation.
- ☐ The Board supports the CEO/CAO/ED through ongoing feedback, professional development and appropriate recognition.

Rate your **overall performance** over the past 2-3 years against this Practice Guideline:	Rate the **importance** of practicing this Guideline in your organizational context:
Unacceptable 1 2 3 4 5 6 7 Excellent	Not at all 1 2 3 4 5 6 7 Very
Comments:	Comments:
DK	

Practice Guideline 3.5:
The Board commissions, receives and acts on an annual financial audit of organizational performance.

Quality Indicators to consider prior to rating this Practice Guideline:

☐ The Board appoints an independent auditor annually, with approval granted at the AGM.

☐ The Board appoints an audit committee composed of independent board members with appropriate financial expertise.

☐ The Board reviews the financial audit in relation to organizational progress toward desired outcomes.

☐ The Board revisits its long range financial plan upon receipt of each annual audit.

Rate your **overall performance** over the past 2-3 years against this Practice Guideline:	Rate the **importance** of practicing this Guideline in your organizational context:
Unacceptable 1 2 3 4 5 6 7 Excellent	Not at all 1 2 3 4 5 6 7 Very
Comments:	Comments:
DK	

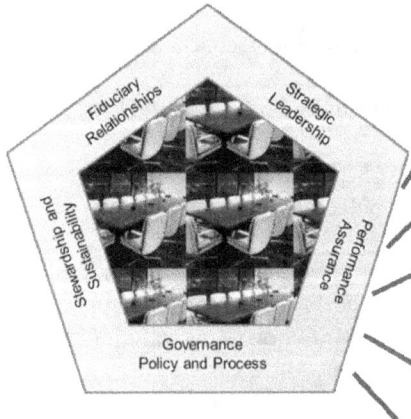

3.1 Building an outcome-driven culture

3.2 Monitoring/evaluating delivery of outcomes

3.3 Regular reports on performance to budget, productivity/efficiency and service quality

3.4 CEO/CAO/ED performance management

3.5 Annual financial audit of organizational performance

4 – Stewardship and Sustainability

Practice Guideline 4.1:
The Board has ensured that policies, long range financial plans, and strategies are in place that realistically provide for the financial resources to support ongoing, sustainable delivery of the organization's promise and potential.

Quality Indicators to consider prior to rating this Practice Guideline:

- ☐ The Board is committed to the development of a strong, diverse and sustainable revenue base.
- ☐ Board policies have been developed that address revenue development, financial management (spending, controls, monitoring), financial risks and investment management.
- ☐ The Board is involved in the development and monitoring of a long range financial plan that provides for the resources required to achieve both operational excellence and exemplary asset management.
- ☐ Annual budgets align with and demonstrate progress towards the long range financial plan.

Rate your **overall performance** over the past 2-3 years against this Practice Guideline: Unacceptable 1 2 3 4 5 6 7 Excellent Comments: DK	Rate the **importance** of practicing this Guideline in your organizational context: Not at all 1 2 3 4 5 6 7 Very Comments:

Practice Guideline 4.2:
The Board takes a leadership role in the organization's fund development program.

Quality Indicators to consider prior to rating this Practice Guideline:

- ☐ Board members are donors themselves, setting an example and demonstrating commitment by contributing regularly to the annual campaign.
- ☐ The Board has set policies, including a gift acceptance policy, which provide guidance to the fund development activity.
- ☐ The Board has input into, and is familiar with, the Case for fundraising.
- ☐ Everyone in a leadership position in the organization knows what the priorities are in the year or two ahead – priorities that need fund development support.
- ☐ The Board is active in the relationship building and stewardship activities necessary to ensure a strong, diverse and sustainable revenue base – government relations, major donor cultivation.
- ☐ Board members participate in the fund development process (input into FD targets/plans, identification of prospects, attending events, making asks, etc.)

Rate your **overall performance** over the past 2-3 years against this Practice Guideline: Unacceptable 1 2 3 4 5 6 7 Excellent Comments: DK	Rate the **importance** of practicing this Guideline in your organizational context: Not at all 1 2 3 4 5 6 7 Very Comments:

Practice Guideline 4.3:
The Board has approved policies that both nurture and protect its human resource assets.

Quality Indicators to consider prior to rating this Practice Guideline:

☐ The board has approved policies that clearly define its expectations related to organizational culture and human resource management.
☐ The policies include commitment to a quality work environment, ongoing professional development, and the safety and security of both staff and volunteers.
☐ Policies have been approved to protect organizational memory and best practice (to protect against loss of key staff).
☐ The Board requires that succession plans or strategies are in place for key staff positions.
☐ The Board has developed succession plans or strategies for key board leadership positions.

Rate your **overall performance** over the past 2-3 years against this Practice Guideline:

Unacceptable   1   2   3   4   5   6   7   Excellent

Comments:

Rate the **importance** of practicing this Guideline in your organizational context:

Not at all   1   2   3   4   5   6   7   Very

Comments:

DK

Practice Guideline 4.4:
The Board has ensured that a comprehensive asset management program is in place – including an asset inventory, preventive maintenance system, and a capital replacement plan.

Quality Indicators to consider prior to rating this Practice Guideline:

☐ The Board reviews the organization's asset inventory, preventive maintenance systems, and capital replacement plans.
☐ The Board has ensured that reserve funding is regularly set aside to support planned major maintenance and capital replacement.
☐ The Board reviews an annual summary of deferred or unfunded required preventive maintenance, including a professional assessment of related impact.

Rate your **overall performance** over the past 2-3 years against this Practice Guideline:

Unacceptable   1   2   3   4   5   6   7   Excellent

Comments:

Rate the **importance** of practicing this Guideline in your organizational context:

Not at all   1   2   3   4   5   6   7   Very

Comments:

DK

Practice Guideline 4.5:
The Board has ensured that processes are in place to evaluate/manage business risk; to minimize both loss and liability; and to ensure the health, safety and security of any persons involved in the organization or its services.

Quality Indicators to consider prior to rating this Practice Guideline:

☐ Directors understand that risk management is a core function of the Board (in partnership with management)
☐ The breadth of risk to the organization is understood and regularly reviewed: compliance risk, data/information risk, asset risk, financial risk, governance risk, operational risk, reputational risk.
☐ The Board has ensured that an overall Risk Management Policy and Plan is in place.
☐ The organization has a business continuity policy and plan in place (disaster recovery).
☐ The Board has approved a risk tolerance policy defining the level of risk that the organization is willing to assume.
☐ The Board and CEO/CAO/ED regularly consult with their insurers to review and update risk coverage related to assets, general liability, and director/officer liability.
☐ Risk assessment is integrated into all major policy development, planning and decision making activities. Directors challenge assumptions behind all recommendations.
☐ The Board develops and refines its understanding of the risks associated with the organization's business and ensures that management has adequate processes in place to address same.
☐ Crisis or issue management policies, procedures and accountabilities are clear.

Rate your **overall performance** over the past 2-3 years against this Practice Guideline: Unacceptable 1 2 3 4 5 6 7 Excellent Comments: DK	Rate the **importance** of practicing this Guideline in your organizational context: Not at all 1 2 3 4 5 6 7 Very Comments:

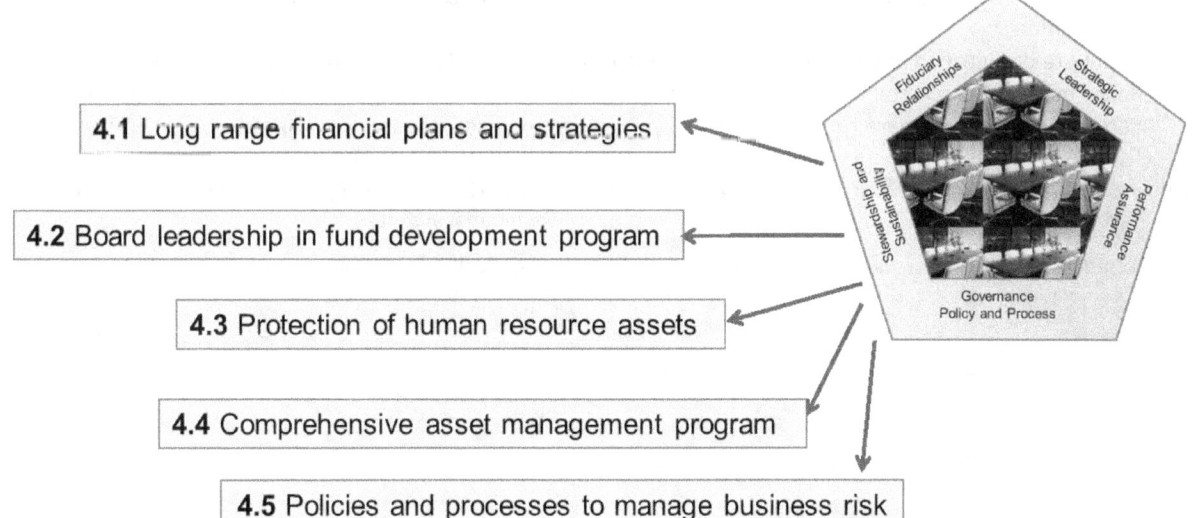

4.1 Long range financial plans and strategies
4.2 Board leadership in fund development program
4.3 Protection of human resource assets
4.4 Comprehensive asset management program
4.5 Policies and processes to manage business risk

5 – Governance Policy and Process

Practice Guideline 5.1:
The Board has developed specific policies and procedures that define how it will address all of its obligations under society law and the bylaws of the organization.

Quality Indicators to consider prior to rating this Practice Guideline:
- ☐ Board obligations are clearly identified and calendared so that Board agendas address each key responsibilities in a timely manner.
- ☐ Responsibility for critical obligations is built into the CEO/ED job description and a compliance check is conducted as part of the annual review process.

Rate your **overall performance** over the past 2-3 years against this Practice Guideline:

Unacceptable 1 2 3 4 5 6 7 Excellent

Comments:

Rate the **importance** of practicing this Guideline in your organizational context:

Not at all 1 2 3 4 5 6 7 Very

Comments:

DK

Practice Guideline 5.2:
The Board has a good understanding of the operational realities facing the organization, a critical foundation to effective decision-making.

Quality Indicators to consider prior to rating this Practice Guideline:
- ☐ A comprehensive and effective orientation process is in place for new Board members
- ☐ Board members take time to familiarize themselves with the services, programs and facilities of the organization
- ☐ Adequate background and contextual information is provided in all reports requiring Board action
- ☐ Board members understand they have the right to be informed and the right to full discussion before decisions are taken. Board reports and decision-making processes respect these rights.

Rate your **overall performance** over the past 2-3 years against this Practice Guideline:

Unacceptable 1 2 3 4 5 6 7 Excellent

Comments:

Rate the **importance** of practicing this Guideline in your organizational context:

Not at all 1 2 3 4 5 6 7 Very

Comments:

DK

Practice Guideline 5.3:
Board membership and makeup supports and aligns with the purpose of the organization.

Quality Indicators to consider prior to rating this Practice Guideline:
- ☐ The Board has a clear strategy for the recruitment, development and retention of Board members qualified to collectively handle Board roles and responsibilities.
- ☐ Board membership is diverse, bringing a range of talents and experience to the table – related to the mandate and risk profile of the organization.
- ☐ Board members are committed to the purpose, mission, vision and values of the organization.
- ☐ Board members are committed to creating value for stakeholders.
- ☐ Board members are influential either in the community to be served or with those in a position to support the work of the organization.
- ☐ Board members are committed to policy governance .
- ☐ Board members are strategic thinkers, financially literate, and relationship builders.
- ☐ A grid is utilized to ensure that current and newly appointed Board members together represent different age and gender perspectives, geographic service areas, cultural backgrounds, and required areas of expertise.
- ☐ The Board completes a formal assessment of members skill sets annually and adjusts its recruitment and Board development strategies accordingly.

Rate your **overall performance** over the past 2-3 years against this Practice Guideline:

Unacceptable   1   2   3   4   5   6   7   Excellent

Comments:

DK

Rate the **importance** of practicing this Guideline in your organizational context:

Not at all   1   2   3   4   5   6   7   Very

Comments:

Practice Guideline 5.4:
The Board has clearly defined the respective roles and responsibilities of the Board and management and knows when to delegate or transfer responsibility and accountability to the CEO/CAO/ED.

Quality Indicators to consider prior to rating this Practice Guideline:
- ☐ A policy is in place that clarifies the types of decisions to be made by the Board AND those that can be made by the CEO/CAO/ED.
- ☐ This policy also clarifies when input from other levels (e.g. committees, staff, finance officer, etc.) is required prior to a decision being taken; responsibility for implementation or executive of the decision; and responsibility for monitoring to ensure compliance.
- ☐ Written job descriptions are provided for all board positions and committees.

Rate your **overall performance** over the past 2-3 years against this Practice Guideline:

Unacceptable   1   2   3   4   5   6   7   Excellent

Comments:

DK

Rate the **importance** of practicing this Guideline in your organizational context:

Not at all   1   2   3   4   5   6   7   Very

Comments:

Practice Guideline 5.5:
Board meetings are structured so as to make room for critical Board work as defined in this handbook.

Quality Indicators to consider prior to rating this Practice Guideline:
- ☐ Agendas are structured to make time for work in the areas of strategic leadership, performance assurance, and sustainability/stewardship.
- ☐ Board agendas also focus on strategic priorities and emerging issues/opportunities of strategic import.
- ☐ Information items and updates are circulated prior to meetings and only addressed at the meeting if Board members raise issues or questions of strategic import.
- ☐ Longer meetings are scheduled periodically to provide for the depth of discussion required before major decisions are taken.

Rate your **overall performance** over the past 2-3 years against this Practice Guideline:

Unacceptable 1 2 3 4 5 6 7 Excellent

Comments:

DK

Rate the **importance** of practicing this Guideline in your organizational context:

Not at all 1 2 3 4 5 6 7 Very

Comments:

Practice Guideline 5.6:
Board committees are established to support the governance roles of the Board, not to duplicate management functions.

Quality Indicators to consider prior to rating this Practice Guideline:
- ☐ The few standing committees of the Board relate to the core competencies suggested here: fiduciary relationships, strategic leadership, performance assurance, stewardship/sustainability, development, and governance.
- ☐ Shorter term teams or task forces are assembled from time to time to address and support the strategic priorities of the organization.
- ☐ Committees that reflect management functions (e.g. finance, HR, marketing/communications, programs) are generally avoided with any Board fiduciary obligations in these areas handled through Performance Assurance or Stewardship/Sustainability in a comprehensive manner.

Rate your **overall performance** over the past 2-3 years against this Practice Guideline:

Unacceptable 1 2 3 4 5 6 7 Excellent

Comments:

DK

Rate the **importance** of practicing this Guideline in your organizational context:

Not at all 1 2 3 4 5 6 7 Very

Comments:

Practice Guideline 5.7:
Board culture and behaviour optimizes the contribution of each board member.

Quality Indicators to consider prior to rating this Practice Guideline:
- ☐ The Board has developed clear and effective decision-making processes.
- ☐ The Board operates under a shared leadership model that both optimizes individual contribution and Board capacity to deliver on its promise.
- ☐ Board members have sufficient information to make informed decisions.
- ☐ The majority of Board meetings allow for and support open discussion of strategic issues.
- ☐ Meetings are managed so as to ensure full participation of all Board members, avoiding domination by a small number of individuals.
- ☐ Regular debriefs are held to reflect on and improve Board participation and decision-making processes.

Rate your **overall performance** over the past 2-3 years against this Practice Guideline:

Unacceptable 1 2 3 4 5 6 7 Excellent

Comments:

Rate the **importance** of practicing this Guideline in your organizational context:

Not at all 1 2 3 4 5 6 7 Very

Comments:

DK

Practice Guideline 5.8:
The Board is committed to ongoing Board development.

Quality Indicators to consider prior to rating this Practice Guideline:
- ☐ A formal Board development program is crafted, approved and implemented each year.
- ☐ Plans and strategies are developed to address significant issues identified during the Board evaluation process.
- ☐ At least once annually, a Board development session is planned to help build the competencies discussed in this book.
- ☐ Individual behaviour problems are addressed in a direct, confidential and constructive manner, never ignored.

Rate your **overall performance** over the past 2-3 years against this Practice Guideline:

Unacceptable 1 2 3 4 5 6 7 Excellent

Comments:

Rate the **importance** of practicing this Guideline in your organizational context:

Not at all 1 2 3 4 5 6 7 Very

Comments:

DK

Practice Guideline 5.9:
The Board monitors governance literature and takes the time to periodically reflect on and enhance its own governance approach or model.

Quality Indicators to consider prior to rating this Practice Guideline:
- ☐ The Board takes an active interest in governance theory and best practice with a view to improving its own performance.
- ☐ From time to time, the Board asks a committee to review current thinking on effective governance and bring forward appropriate recommendations.
- ☐ Board commitment to learning about governance is reflected in the Board development plan.

Rate your **overall performance** over the past 2-3 years against this Practice Guideline:	Rate the **importance** of practicing this Guideline in your organizational context:
Unacceptable 1 2 3 4 5 6 7 Excellent	Not at all 1 2 3 4 5 6 7 Very
Comments:	Comments:
DK	

Practice Guideline 5.10:
The Board conducts regular assessments of its own performance and takes appropriate corrective action when issues are identified.

Quality Indicators to consider prior to rating this Practice Guideline:
- ☐ An annual Board self-assessment is conducted that is largely focused on the extent to which Board competencies and required practices are addressed.
- ☐ This self-assessment is complemented by conduct of a number of one-on-one interviews to obtain feedback from senior management, funders, partner organizations, client spokespersons, etc.
- ☐ The performance of individual directors is evaluated each year using a facilitated and confidential peer-review survey
- ☐ Provision is made for annual evaluation of the performance of each board committee.
- ☐ Action plans are developed to ensure that identified board performance issues are addressed.

Rate your **overall performance** over the past 2-3 years against this Practice Guideline:	Rate the **importance** of practicing this Guideline in your organizational context:
Unacceptable 1 2 3 4 5 6 7 Excellent	Not at all 1 2 3 4 5 6 7 Very
Comments:	Comments:
DK	

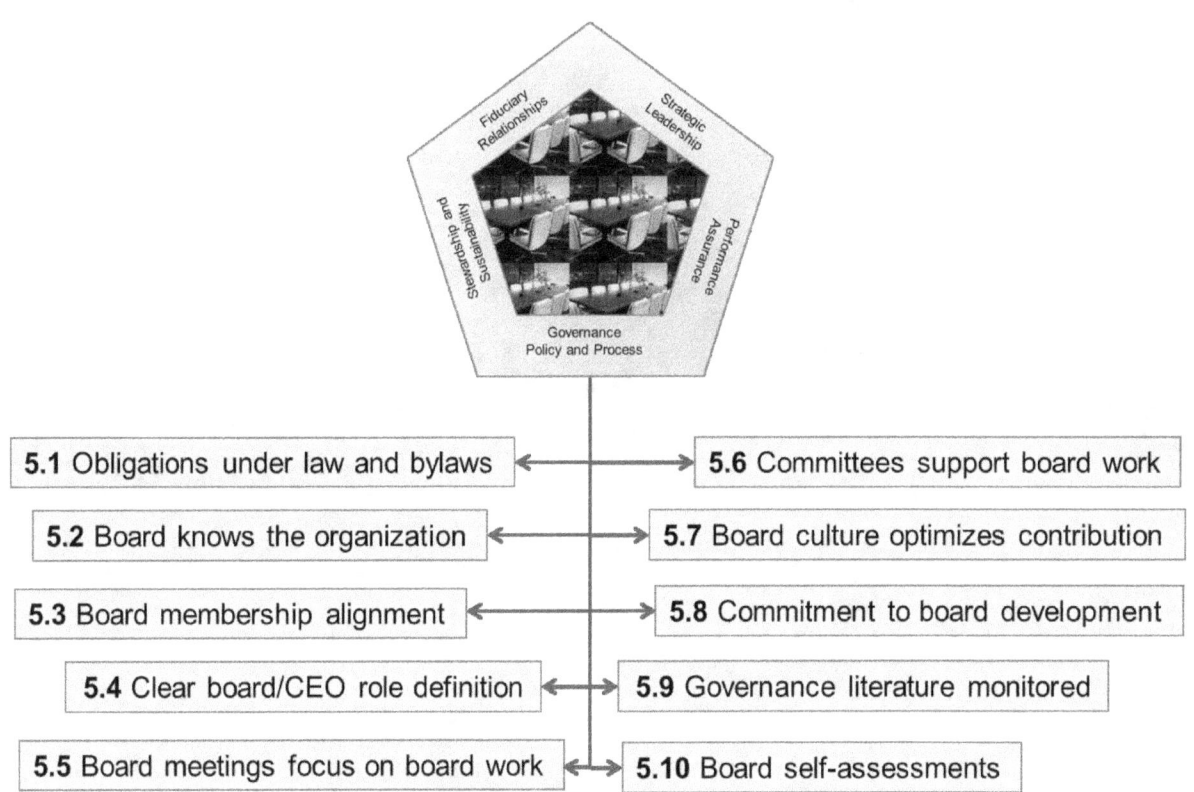

5.1 Obligations under law and bylaws	**5.6** Committees support board work
5.2 Board knows the organization	**5.7** Board culture optimizes contribution
5.3 Board membership alignment	**5.8** Commitment to board development
5.4 Clear board/CEO role definition	**5.9** Governance literature monitored
5.5 Board meetings focus on board work	**5.10** Board self-assessments

Section 3:

The Assessment Process

Dimensions of Use

This governance self-assessment tool can be used in a number of ways. Dimensions to consider before you begin the process include:

- Overall purpose - whether you are looking for a quick assessment, an opportunity for discussion/reflection, or a comprehensive, in-depth evaluation
- The number and type of individuals to involve in the assessment process
- Whether your process will be opinion-based or evidence-based
- The objectivity required of the reviewer or analyst
- Methods of data collection and analysis, and
- How findings will be ultimately used or presented.

The table below explores some of the options involved.

Dimension	Options
Purpose	• Take an hour or so on your own, to remind yourself of some of the basic governance practices and ask if your team needs to do something more, or something different • Consider using the assessment as a team building exercise – a discussion starter that will have many benefits • Others may see this as an infrequent opportunity to step back and have a careful look at your entire governance culture with the intent of making significant change or improvement (if required).
Who should be involved	• The smaller the team that uses the assessment tool, the more likely that participants will be close to and knowledgeable about the organization and its governance practices. It is also relatively easy to discuss findings, agree on implications and design follow-up action. Any potentially awkward findings can be kept relatively low profile while you are addressing the gap or issue identified. • The larger the reach, the more people you involve, the more you will be dealing with arms-length perspectives and will get many more DK (don't know) responses. However, a broader process will educate key individuals about governance, identify areas where additional education is required, and would build relationships between your board and key stakeholders. • If this is your first significant governance review, it may be best to limit the assessment and discussion process to board members and the Executive Director, CAO or CEO.

Dimension	Options
Opinion-Based or Evidence-Based	• The assessment may be conducted relying on the opinions and current level of awareness of participants. This may result in many DK (don't know) responses, which is in itself useful information. • Provision of some basic information showing evidence of board performance against each governance competency domain or practice guideline will reduce the DK responses, but inevitably bias the rating response somewhat. This approach will make it more difficult for participants to give high ratings in an area where there is no documentation of previous performance. • The initial use of the assessment tool could be opinion based, with later assessments assisted by developing evidence files for each Governance Competency Domain, possibly adding external peer review in some way.
Objectivity	• The internal team can do the evaluation carrying a dual risk – those with 'glass half full' personalities will inevitably be more complementary than those who are looking for problems to solve ('glass half empty). • Use of an external facilitator can enhance both the credibility of the process and the quality of debate/discussion along the way.
Methods of Data Collection and Analysis	• Hand tabulation of paper assessment forms is always an option. • The data may also be entered into a spreadsheet so that more sophisticated calculations can be done and graphics easily produced. • An online survey can also be used to facilitate both collection and analysis of the data – particularly useful if cross tabulation is required for larger numbers of participants (Survey Monkey support can be provided by authors).
Ultimate use of Assessment Results	• If the results are intended for internal team review and discussion, there will be a tendency to select the simpler options listed toward the top of each cell in this table. This will also be true if the results are intended to feed into a larger process such as a Strategic Plan or organization-wide performance management process. • However, if the assessment results will be presented formally to a larger audience (e.g. full membership, cross section of stakeholders), there will a tendency to adopt process options toward the bottom of each of the above cells. The more transparent the process, the greater the need to be thorough, comprehensive and credible.

Generalized Process Suggestions

Phase	Steps
Preparation	• Appoint an 'Assessment Coordinator' to provide leadership and handle mechanics during the process. • Team Orientation – meet with the team involved to introduce the purpose, process and how you intend to use the results. Be open to suggestions. • Collect any background material required if you have decided on an 'evidence based' approach. • Encourage assessment participants to read the front end of this book and glance over the assessment tool by way of additional orientation. • Customize the Assessment Tool so that it looks like your organization (logo, rephrasing to use language comfortable to your organization).
Distribution and Return	• Finalize list of participants in the assessment process – a spreadsheet with contact information. • Draft an advance email, fax or letter designed to motivate participation and letting them know when to expect the assessment tool. This is particularly important if you have decided to use an online survey so that the request is not sidelined to the 'junk email basket'. Be clear on timelines – when the assessment is due back. Make a commitment to confidentiality (data and comments will be used but not attributed to an individual). • Keep a record of who has returned the assessment and send out a reminder to those who have not responded a few days before final closing or due date. Personalize this if possible.

Analysis of Feedback
 	
additional detail provided on following pages
	• At a minimum, calculate the mean and standard deviation for the two ratings for each of the 30 Practice Guidelines.
	
	• Assuming that the volume of related comments permits, for each of the Practice Guidelines:
	    ○ Group similar comments
	    ○ Capture the essence of each cluster using the best wording provided by participants
	    ○ Place a number in parentheses after this summary statement that shows the number of individuals that made a similar comment.
	
	• Using the means, plot the relative position of each Practice Guideline on a graphic that uses the importance rating as the vertical scale and the performance rating as the horizontal scale. See following pages for examples.

Phase	Steps

Discussion	- Congratulate the team on all Practice Guidelines where performance was scored with a mean of 6 or higher (right quadrants of the graphics).
	
	- Have a close look at any Practice Guidelines (PGs) that had importance ratings of 5-7 (relatively high) with performance ratings of 1-3 (relatively low). These will be the PGs that appear in the top left quadrant of the graphics for each of the five Governance Competency Domains. Review comments, discuss optional responses for addressing these potential performance gaps. Reflect on:
	    - whether or not the overall governance team appreciates the importance of this practice
	    - what initiatives or interventions have been tried in this practice area over the past couple of years.
	    - what can be done in the upcoming year to improve performance in this practice area (e.g. improved orientation, protecting time for the governance function, establishing a task team to look into it).
	
	- If there are relatively few PGs in the top left quadrant, return to the top right quadrant and look at Practice Guidelines that had high importance scores but average performance scores (4 or 5 on the 7-point scale).
	
	- Have a quick look at any Practice Guidelines that appear in the lower two quadrants to make sure the team is comfortable with reasons given (comments) for these PGs not being important to governance in your organization.
	
	- Finally, review the number of DK responses (don't know) to identify areas where additional board orientation, information or development work may be required in the future.

Follow-Up	- Report back to all participants with a summary of findings. - Develop an action plan to address each Practice Guideline that needs attention in the year or two ahead. Example format provided on following pages. - Review progress on action plans and take corrective steps as necessary to support the required work.

Graphic Summary of Assessments

After you have completed 30 assessment ratings, review your ratings one Governance Domain at a time. An example follows:

- For the Fiduciary Relations GCD (Governance Competency Domain), you will have five pairs of ratings –for each of the Practice Guidelines you will have one rating for importance, and a second for performance

- Use the first graphic on the next page to plot your rating for the first Practice Guideline (PG) –
    - You are going to place a '1.1' (for the first guideline) on the two-scale graphic
    - A performance rating of 6 and an importance rating of 6 will place this '1.1' roughly in the middle of the top right quadrant
    - A performance rating of 3 and an importance rating of 6 would place the '1.2' in the middle of the top left quadrat.

- Place all five of the Practice Guideline numbers on the Fiduciary Relationship graphic

- Repeat this for the remaining four Governance Competency Domains.

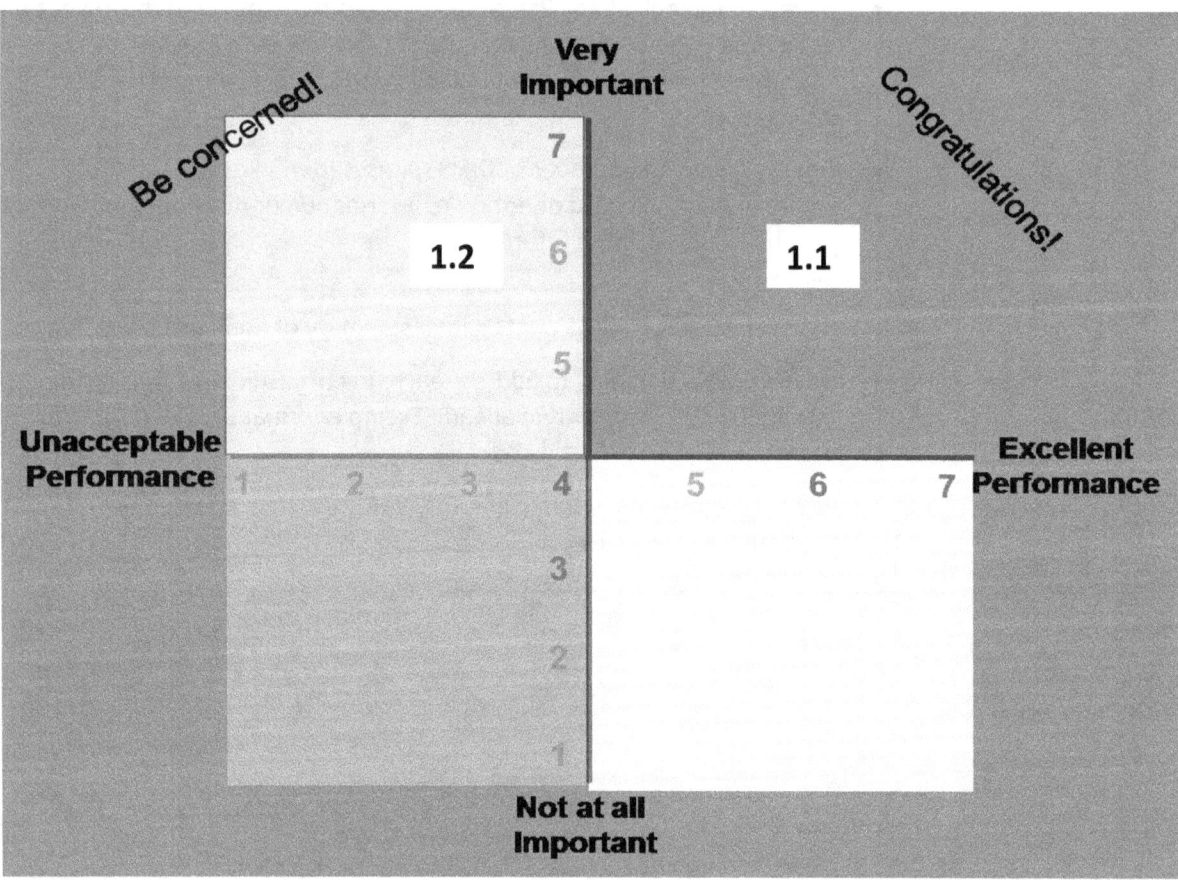

54

Fiduciary Relationships

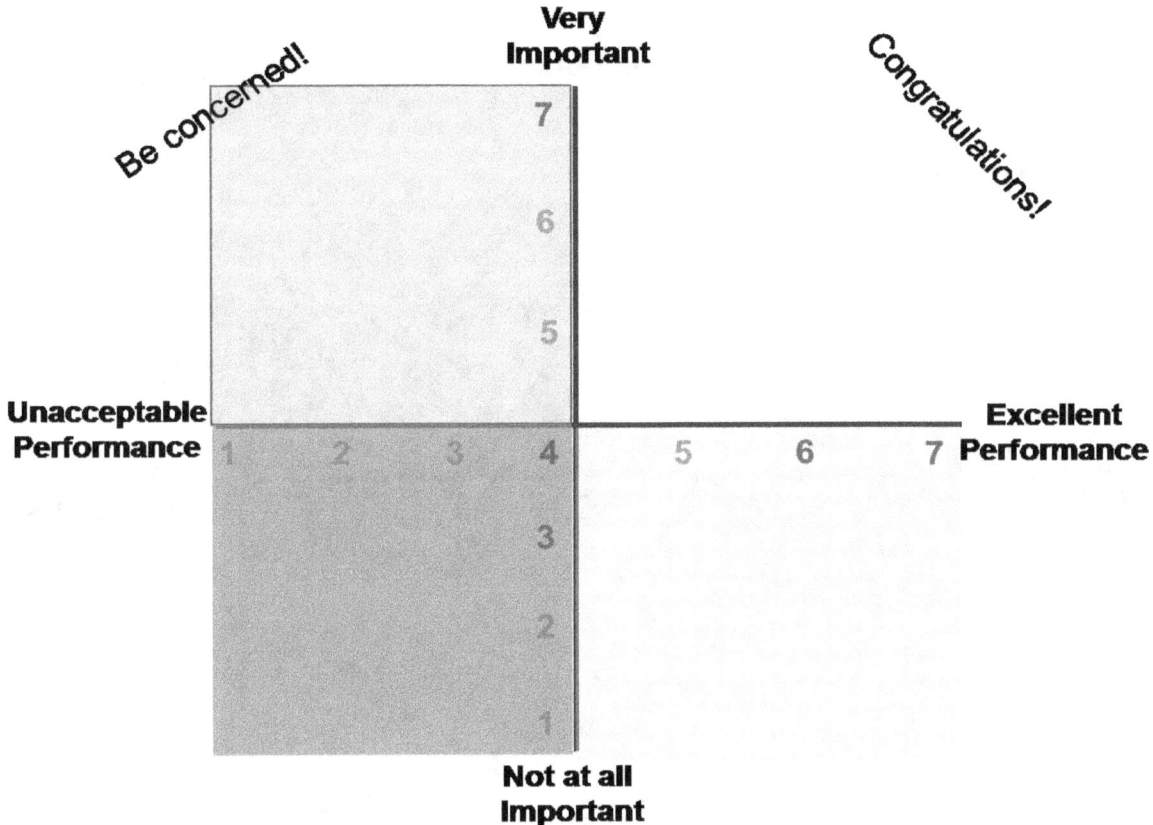

1.1 Clear accountability to owners and stakeholders

1.2 Ability to identify priority needs, concerns and issues

1.3 Decision making considers stakeholder interests

1.4 Board engages and reports regularly to stakeholders

1.5 Board relations with other organizations serving similar clients and stakeholders

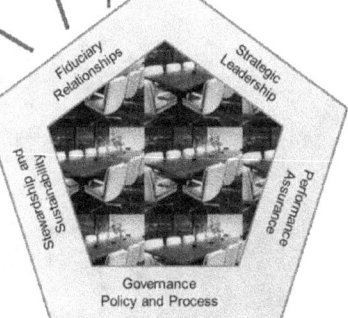

Strategic Leadership

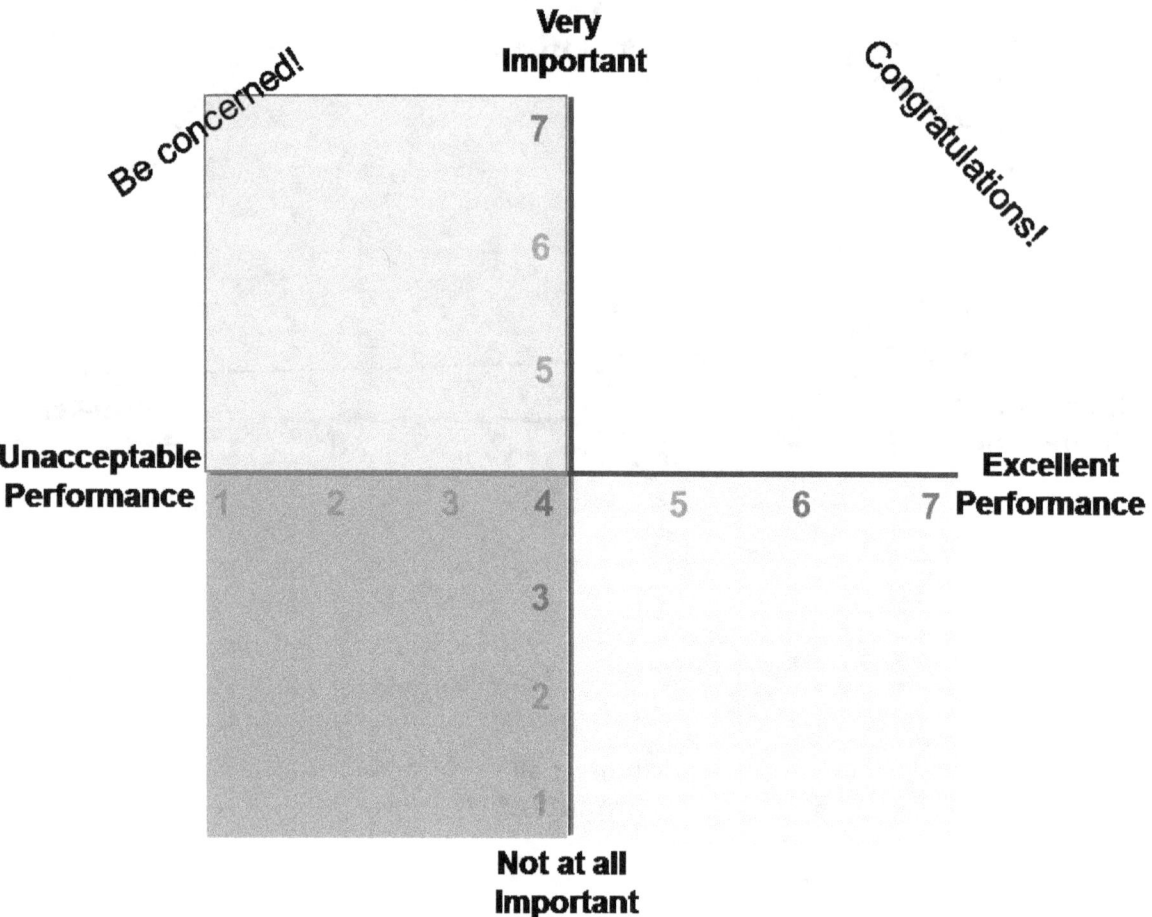

2.1 Clear purpose, vision, focus and perimeter of concern

2.2 Well defined priorities and strategic direction

2.3 Support for constant improvement and innovation

2.4 Champion of the organization's brand and reputation

2.5 Development/refinement of organizational strategy

Performance Assurance

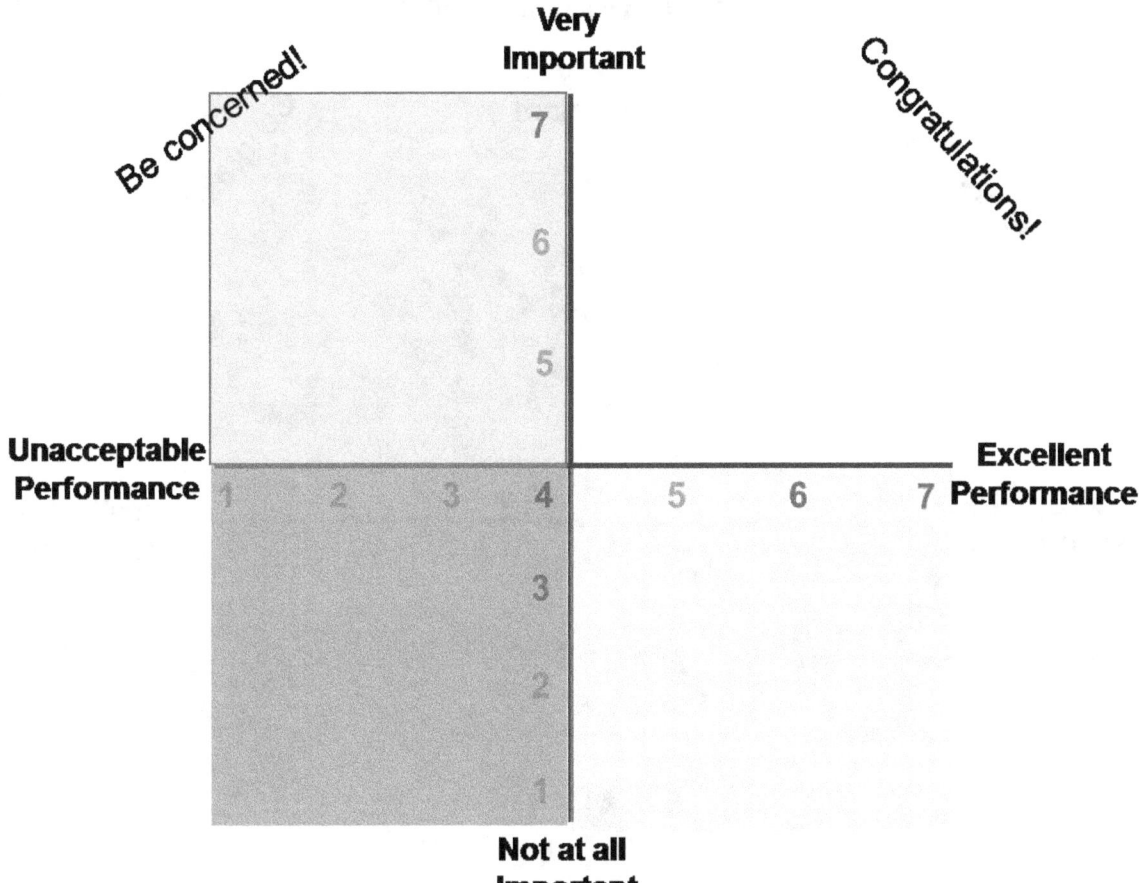

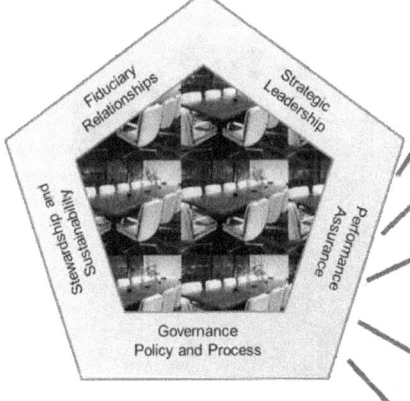

3.1 Building an outcome-driven culture

3.2 Monitoring/evaluating delivery of outcomes

3.3 Regular reports on performance to budget, productivity/efficiency and service quality

3.4 CEO/CAO/ED performance management

3.5 Annual financial audit of organizational performance

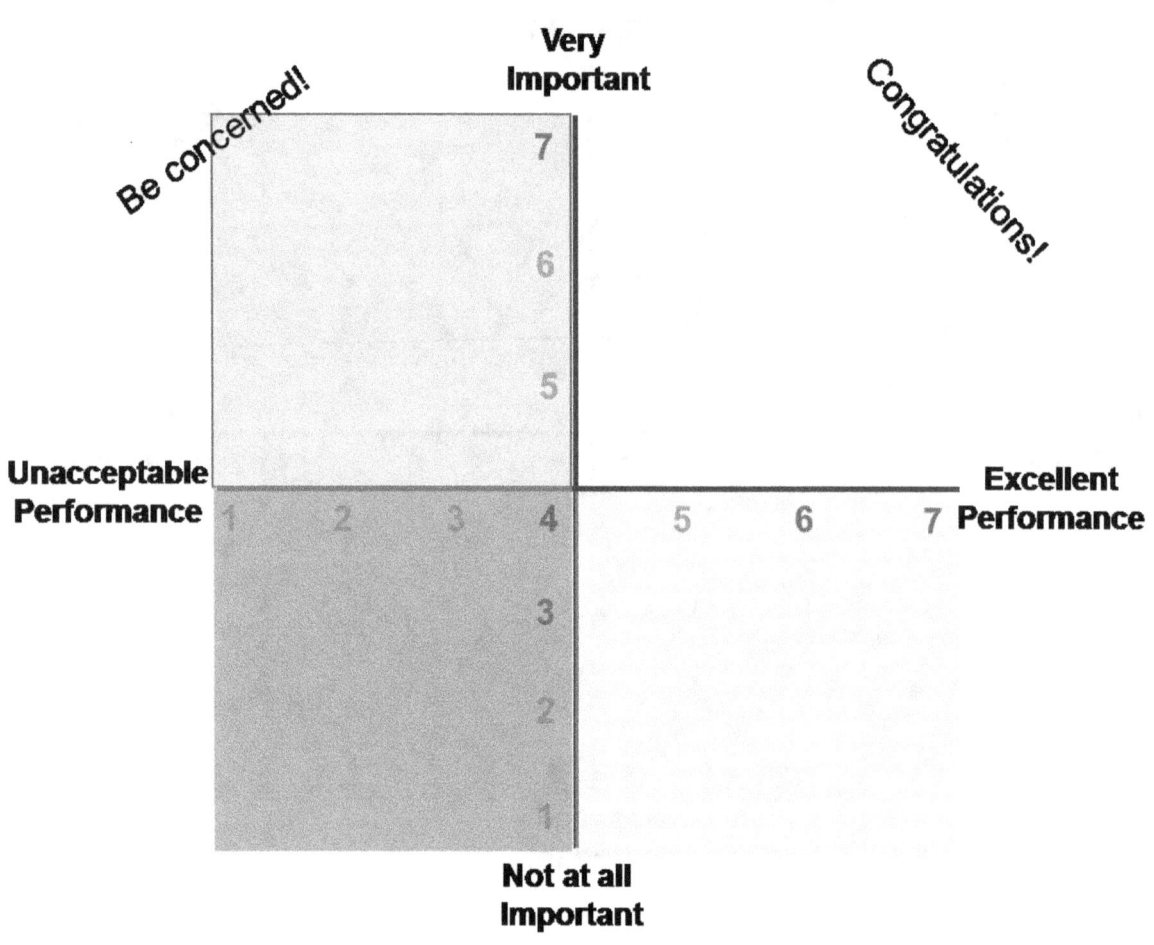

Stewardship and Sustainability

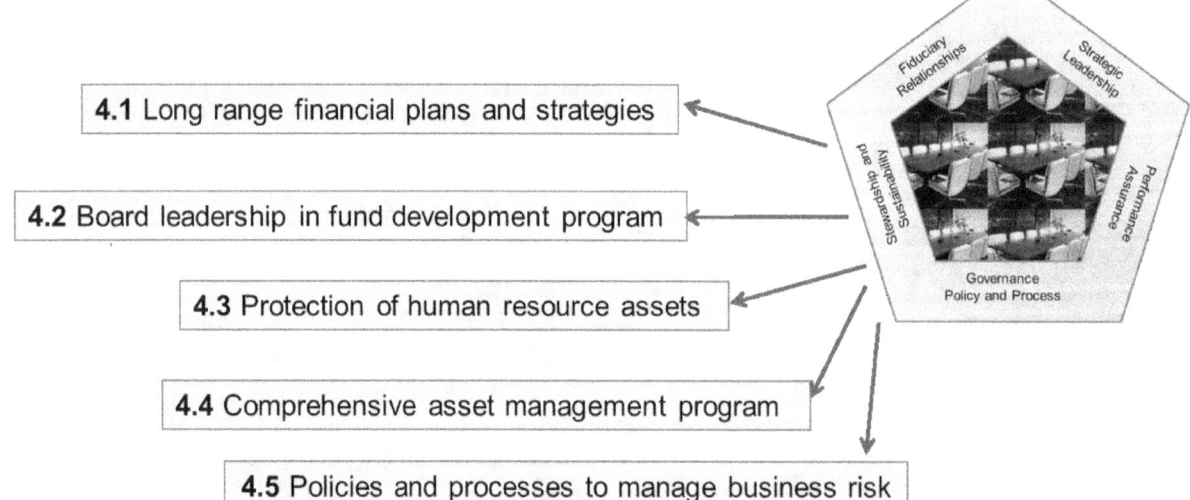

4.1 Long range financial plans and strategies

4.2 Board leadership in fund development program

4.3 Protection of human resource assets

4.4 Comprehensive asset management program

4.5 Policies and processes to manage business risk

Governance Policy and Process

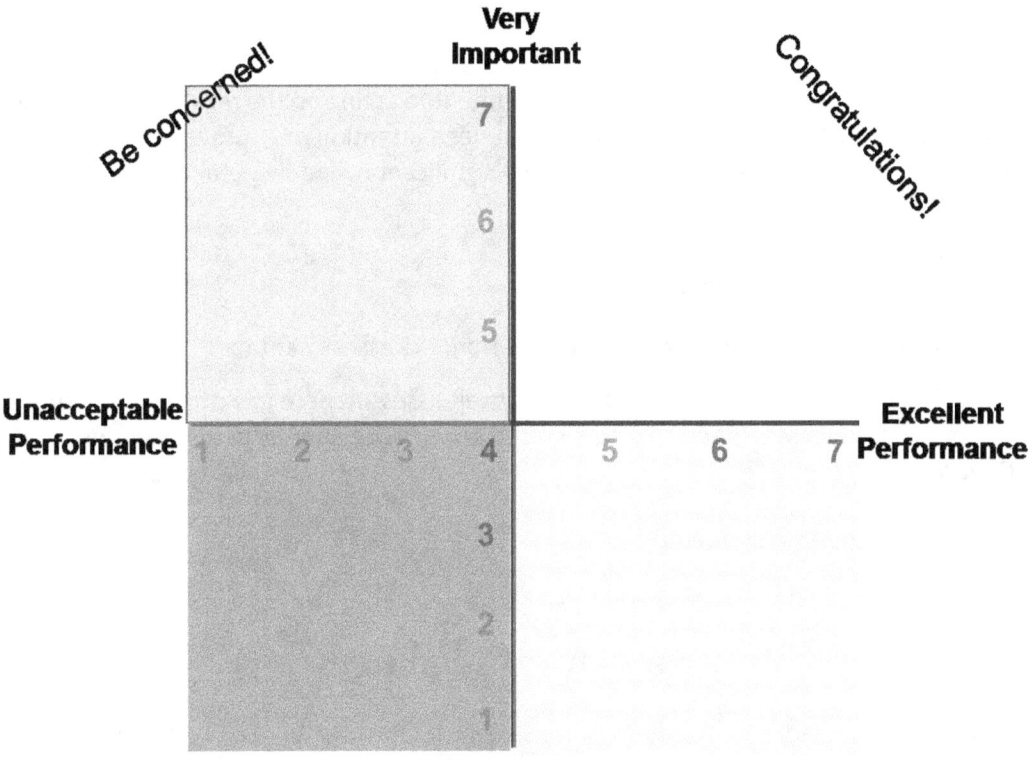

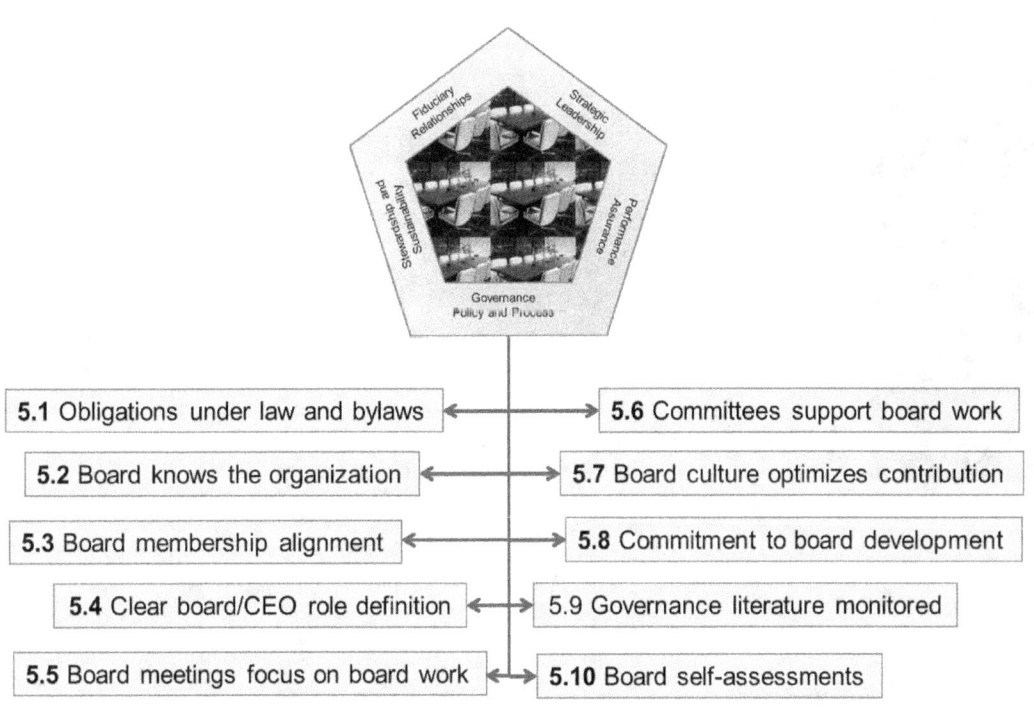

5.1 Obligations under law and bylaws	5.6 Committees support board work
5.2 Board knows the organization	5.7 Board culture optimizes contribution
5.3 Board membership alignment	5.8 Commitment to board development
5.4 Clear board/CEO role definition	5.9 Governance literature monitored
5.5 Board meetings focus on board work	5.10 Board self-assessments

Action Plans

It is important to demonstrate organizational commitment to acting on the results of the assessment process. If three or four Practice Guideline areas that need attention or improvement are identified and acted on each year, the cumulative effect will be significant over a five year period.

The area needing attention could relate to:

- a complete Practice Guideline
- a Quality Indicator that you strongly support from the assessment tool
- some larger concept that emerged from your self-assessment (e.g. a commitment to policy governance, a desire to develop a customized governance approach, the need for a Governance Committee).

The following table is offered as a template:

Governance Action Items

Area needing attention	Outcomes/ Results Desired	Steps	By whom	When	Costs

Section 4:

Accountability and Role Clarity

The Challenge

The **RETHINKING Governance** framework identifies 5 Governance Core Competencies, 30 related Practice Guidelines, and 140 Quality Indicators. Once your organization has completed the self-assessment, you will have confirmed a subset of each of the above that your Board believes are important in your context (as determined by high importance ratings).

While the Board is ultimately responsible for ensuring that all governance obligations are met, the reality is that many areas require collaboration involving the Board, its committees, the Executive Director or CEO, and staff. Further discussion is required to identify the critical roles to be played by each:

- who is ultimately responsible – the decision maker or arbiter
- who is required to play a support role and what kind of support – recommendation, implementation/follow-through, monitoring, etc.

Many organizations rely on Board, committee and CEO/CAO/ED job descriptions to provide this clarity. However, the reality is that these roles are often highly generalized and do not address the full range of 30 Practice Guidelines outlined in this framework. This lack of clarity inevitably results in role confusion and/or neglect of critical governance responsibilities.

Lacking clear board 'marching orders' that clearly define a substantial amount of governance work, the directors may easily slip towards reactionary, oversight or other roles that tend to duplicate management functions. The Board must identify how it wants to engage in each of the practices identified in the 30 Practice Guidelines; clarifying how much authority it desires in each case.

The IRDEM Model

The authors have created/utilized a role clarification model in many organizations to address the abovementioned challenge. The IRDEM Model:

- identifies areas where role confusion may occur (rows in a matrix)
- lists those positions or team involved in the role confusion (columns), and
- assigns a 'responsibility code' in each cell of the resulting table – I for optional input, R for required recommendation prior to decision, D for decision-making authority, E for execution responsibility, and M for monitoring.

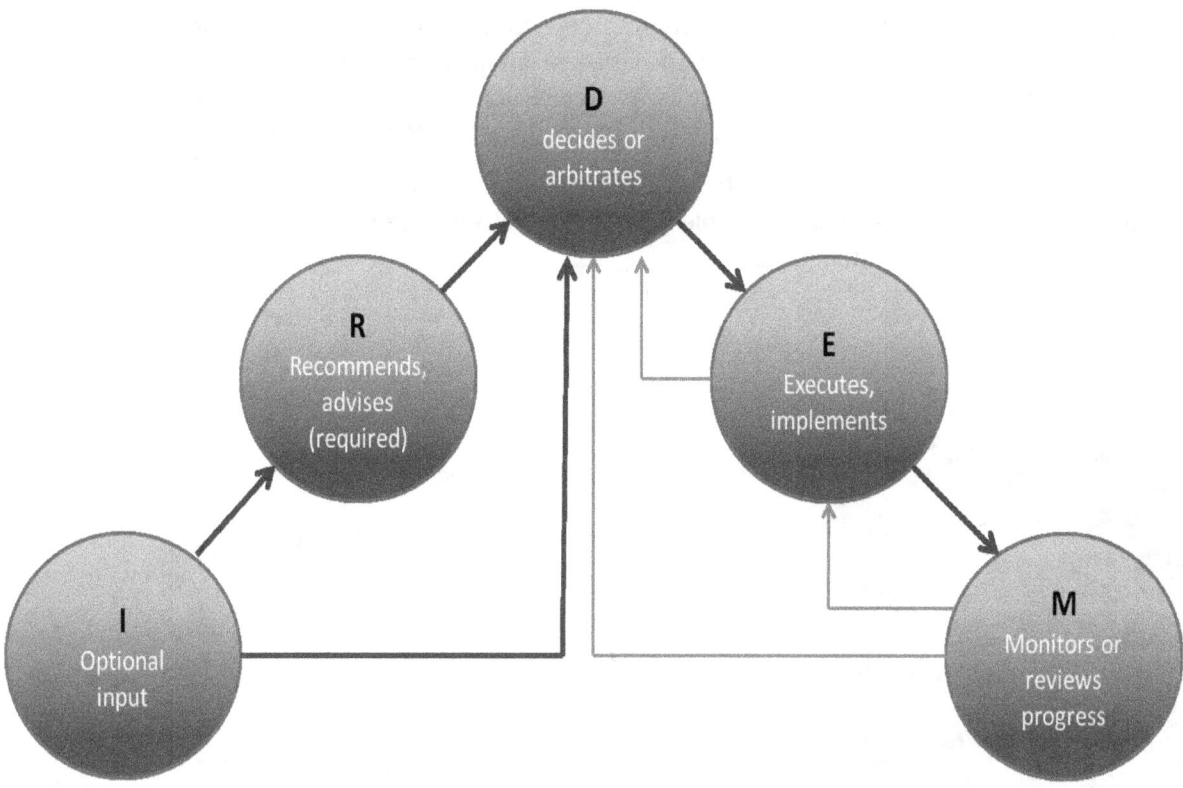

The role/responsibility codes are identified in the above graphic:

- **I** is used to identify those individuals or groups that are invited to provide input to the process prior to a decision being taken – this input is optional and the decision can be taken whether or not the invited party participates

- **R** identifies the individual or team that MUST be involved in development of the recommendation prior to the decision being taken – required recommendation or advice
    - if a report is required (e.g. draft budget, draft plan, formal board report), an upper case 'R' can be used
    - a lower case 'r' can indicate that the team assigned the D will do the work but is required to consult with or have input from another individual or team prior to closure

- **D** identifies the individual or team that must make the decision – the arbiter

- **E** is used to identify those who will be primarily responsible for execution or implementation after the decision is taken

- **M** identifies the individual or team who will take primary responsibility for monitoring and reviewing follow-up and progress related to the decision – ensuring accountability and performance to decision, strategy or plan.

When developing the IRDEM Table or Chart, it is generally advisable to start the discussion by placing the D (for decision-maker) first.

This role clarification tool can be used without reference to the **RETHINKING Governance** framework by identifying obvious areas of current role confusion to initiative the process. Examples are provided below to illustrate how the IRDEM model is completed. Later in this section, the model will be linked to the Governance Competency Domains as a supplementary tool to the self-assessment process.

The first example assumes that the Board must approve an annual budget but does not meet frequently enough to play a meaningful role in budget monitoring, leaving this key role to the Treasurer or Finance Committee.

	Board	Executive Committee	Other Board Committees	ED/CEO	Other
Budget Development	D	r	r Finance	R	
Budget Control and Management			M Finance	D/M	E Finance Officer/ Managers
Hiring/Supervising/ Recognition/Discipline of ED/CEO	R/M	D/E			
Hiring/Supervising/ Recognition/Discipline of Senior Staff		M/I	I	D/E	

The second example (below) could relate to a Board that meets monthly and for various reasons desires a strong role in monitoring the organization's financial situation. It also introduces the possibility of an additional code – SO for 'sign off'; for example the decision to hire the CEO/CAO/ED sits with the Executive Committee, but must be endorsed by the Board as a whole. Needless to say, other configurations are also possible and can be considered.

	Board	Executive Committee	Other Board Committees	ED/CEO	Other
Budget Development	D	r	r Finance	R	
Budget Control and Management	m		m Finance	D/M	E Finance Officer/ Managers
Hiring/Supervising/ Recognition/Discipline of ED/CEO	SO/M	D/E	I		
Hiring/Supervising/ Recognition/Discipline of Senior Staff		M/I	I	D/E	

The following IRDEM table links to the essential elements of the **Rethinking Governance** framework or model. It provides an example only; individual organizations will customize virtually all aspects of the table depending on: the Practice Guidelines that they feel are most important in their context, their organizational structure, their current stance on policy governance.

GOVERNANCE ROLE POLICY OVERVIEW
Example using 'RETHINKING Governance' Framework

I – optional input (invited, not required before a decision is taken); **R** - recommends/advises/consults (required prior to decision); **D** – responsible for final decision; **E** – responsible for execution or implementation; **M** - responsible for monitoring/reviewing to maintain quality, consistency, compliance; **SO** – 'sign off' required before decision is final. Note that a lower case 'r' may be used to suggest required input to another office who will finalize the recommendation (R).

General Role	Specific Function	Board	Exec. Com.	Other Board Com.	ED/CEO	Other	Comments
Fiduciary Relationships Intent is to govern with an understanding and accountability to the needs and interests of stakeholders.	Identification of **PRIORITY NEEDS, CONCERNS** and **ISSUES** of key stakeholder/ customer constituencies	D		R special task team	R	R	Based on an annual survey or other contact with key constituency groups
	Board **DECISION MAKING** considers stakeholder interests	D		R obligation to consult	R	I	ED/CEO responsible for informing relevant constituency groups when major decision are 'in the works'
	Board **REPORTS REGULARLY** to stakeholders	D	r	r	R/E		Minimum requirement of annual report
Strategic Leadership Intent is to become known for the collective ability to focus on what really matters and strive together for excellence.	**HIGH LEVEL POLICY** - Development of mission, vision, values statements - and definition of core businesses	D	M	r/E	r/E/M		Board and ED/CEO share responsibility for monitoring and developing ability to perform to mandate
	Development of **OUTCOME STATEMENTS** that define the results desired for clients, the community and the organization.	D	r/M	r/E/M	r/E		Board and ED/CEO share responsibility for monitoring and enhancing ability of organization to achieve desired results

General Role	Specific Function	Board	Exec. Com.	Other Board Com.	ED/ CEO	Other	Comments
	Prepare overall **STRATEGIC PLAN** capturing all of above and identifying strategic priorities facing the organization	D	E/M	I/E	R/E		
	Development of **Organizational STRATEGY**	I	R		D	R senior staff	Requires a formal investigation from time to time, with partners
	Preparation, monitoring, evaluation of **OPERATIONAL & BUSINESS PLANS** to determine how best to act on overall Strategic Plan, deliver desired outcomes, and allocate resources.	I	M	I/M	D/E	R Senior staff	Board generally receives a business plan for information and is invited to comment based on their expectations, experience and insights.
Performance Assurance Intent is to ensure effective/efficient management, governance and stakeholder accountability.	BUDGET DEVELOPMENT	D	R	R finance	R		
	BUDGET CONTROL and MANAGEMENT			M finance	D/M	E managers	
	Developing the **PERFORMANCE MANAGEMENT SYSTEM** - An integrated system that monitors organization, department and individual performance (outcomes, outputs, efficiency, quality)	D	R	R	R	I Funders and partners	

General Role	Specific Function	Board	Exec. Com.	Other Board Com.	ED/ CEO	Other	Comments
	Managing and implementing the **PERFORMANCE MANAGEMENT SYSTEM** – measuring/ monitoring key indicators, MIS, timely/appropriate reporting of results.	M/D D - acting on poor performance	M	M	E/M/D D implies acting on poor performance		Important that monitoring reports are carefully reviewed and that identified issues be acted on
	MANAGEMENT OF Executive Director/CEO (hiring, supervision, evaluation, recognition, development, discipline, termination, succession planning)	r/SO/M	D/M/E	I			
	ANNUAL AUDIT or Review	D	M		I	R External firm	
Stewardship and Sustainability Intent is to effectively allocate resources to outcome-driven priorities while maintaining fiduciary responsibility and sustainable operations.	Development of a long range **FINANCIAL STRATEGY AND PLAN** – includes identification of growth areas, implications of cost drivers and revenue generation strategies.	D	r/M	r	R/E/M		Board assisted in its fiduciary responsibilities by the Treasurer and Finance Committee
	Development of **HR POLICIES and PROCEDURES** (organizational values/culture, recruitment, job definition, orientation, compensation, benefits, supervision, evaluation, recognition, development, etc.)	R	R/M	I	D/E		

General Role	Specific Function	Board	Exec. Com.	Other Board Com.	ED/ CEO	Other	Comments
	SUCCESSION PLANNING and protection of organizational memory	D for GM			D for staff		
	Development of a comprehensive **ASSET MANAGEMENT PROGRAM**	R note D for funding	R/M	I	D/E/M		The Board will have a **D** for decision to provide adequate funding to support the Asset Management Program.
	Development of a **RISK MANAGEMENT STRATEGY**	R note D for funding	R/M	I	D/E/M		
Governance Policy Intent is to support a policy governance board that effectively deals with its key roles and obligations	Development/maintenance of **GOVERNANCE MANUAL**	D	R	I	R		
	BOARD DEVELOPMENT	D	R/E	r	r		
	BOARD EVALUATION	R	D/E	R	R		

Note: the above IRDEM model mirrors the Governance Competency Domains in the **RETHINKING Governance** framework. Other roles will likely have to be added to comprehensively define board roles in your organization. Addition roles/rows could relate to:

- Communications (branding, key message definition, critical incident management, etc.)
- Capital Projects (initial approval, project management, etc.)
- Various dimensions of fund development
- Program/service development and delivery
- and others.

The Board Calendar

In addition to the IRDEM model, it is advisable to develop a Board Calendar for the year ahead to ensure that:

- key board work is handled on a timely basis
- key board responsibilities and obligations are addressed annually, and
- Board meeting time is devoted first and foremost to Board roles and responsibilities.

An example follows for an organization that meets monthly with a standard calendar year budget cycle. The message is clear: there is lots for the Board to do and actually very little time for the more traditional, hands-on activity.

Month	Board Activity or Decisions required related to:	Prep Responsibility:
January	- new Board member orientation - signing authority renewal - Committee appointments	Executive Committee Executive Committee Executive Committee
February	- Program and Service Review – activities, issues, funding, performance feedback on previous year end results	Executive Director and senior staff
March	- Review/update of Board Manual, governance policy	Governance Committee
April	- Review of Fund Development policy, resources and related initiatives – update FD Plan	Executive Director and Fundraising Committee
May	- Annual Environmental Scan – including assessment of Priority Unmet Needs	Executive Director
June	- Annual budget review and guidelines for next year - Review and refine long range financial plan (cost and revenue)	Treasurer, ED, Exec. Treasurer, ED, Exec.
September	- Reporting/review of Performance Data (as base for update of Strategic Plan and community reporting) - Workshop to review and update Strategic Plan - Approval of Annual Budget	Performance Assurance Committee Governance Committee Treasurer, ED, Executive
October	- Approval of updated Strategic Plan - Annual Audit or External Assessment	Governance Task Team Treasurer, ED, Executive
November	- Annual Report - Board election process and slate	Executive and ED Governance Task Team
December	- Annual Review of Executive Director - Annual Review of Board performance - Annual General Meeting	Executive Committee Governance Task Team Executive and ED

Attachment 1: Sources/References

Brown, Jim, **The Imperfect Board Member** (Jossey-Bass, 2006)

Canadian Coalition for Good Governance, **Building High Performance Boards** (March 2010)

Carver, John and Carver, Miriam, **Reinventing Your Board: A Step-by-Step Guide to Implementing Policy Governance** (San Francisco, Jossey-Bass, 2006)

Certified General Accountants of Ontario, **Grassroots Governance: Governance and the Non-Profit Sector** (2008 ISBN 0-9690132-2-1)

Chait, Richard; Ryan, William; Taylor, Barbara, **Governance as Leadership: Reframing the Work of Nonprofit Boards** (BoardSource Inc., 2005)

Charam, Ram, **Boards That Deliver: Advancing Corporate Governance from Compliance to Competitive Advantage** (Jossey-Bass, 2005)

Deasley, Beth, **Oversight of Risk by the Board of Directors**
http://nonprofitrisk.imaginecanada.ca/files/insuranceinfo/en/publications/beth_deazeley_dec_2009.pdf

Houle, Cyril, **Governing Boards: Their Nature and Nurture** (Washington DC, National Centre for Non-Profit Boards, 1990)

Independent Sector, **Principles for Good Governance and Ethical Practice** (October 2007)
https://www.independentsector.org/uploads/Accountability_Documents/Principles_for_Good_Governance_and_Ethical_Practice.pdf

Institute on Governance, **Basic Role of the Board** http://iog.ca/en/knowledge-areas/board-organizational-governance/basic-role-of-board

McDermott, Will & Emery, **Best Practices: Nonprofit Corporate Governance**
http://www.mwe.com/info/news/wp0604a.pdf

Mollenhauer, Linda, **A Framework for Success for Not-For-Profit Federations** (June 2006, prepared for the Schizophrenia Society of Canada and project partners, ALS Society of Canada and Parkinson Society Canada)

Nadler, David; Behan, Beverly; Nadler, Mark; **Building Better Boards: A Blueprint for Effective Governance** (Jossey-Bass, 2006)

Nelson, Reuben, **New Maps for New Times: A Fresh Look at Persons and Community,** prepared for the National Recreation Summit (Lake Louise, 2011), available through www.lin.ca

Perryman, Gavin, **Fiduciary Responsibility: Why's and What's** (March 2005)
http://www3.telus.net/gavinperryman/Publication%20Articles/fiduciary_responsibility.pdf

Renz, David, **Reframing Governance**, The Nonprofit Quarterly (Winter 2007)

Save the Children, **Governance Best Practice** (London, England)

Society of Corporate Secretaries & Governance Professionals, **Governance for Nonprofit Organizations: From Little Leagues to Big Universities** (New York, 2008)
http://www.governanceprofessionals.org/society/Nonprofits.asp

Strategic Leverage Partners Inc. in partnership with the Centre for Voluntary Sector Research and Development, **National Study of Board Governance Practices in the Non-Profit and Voluntary Sector in Canada** (2006)

www.ingramcontent.com/pod-product-compliance
Lightning Source LLC
Chambersburg PA
CBHW080821170526
45158CB00009B/2488